A Legacy of 21st Century Leadership

A Legacy of 21st Century Leadership

A Guide for Creating a Climate of Leadership Throughout Your Organization

Les Wallace, Ph.D.
James Trinka, Ph.D.

iUniverse, Inc.
New York Lincoln Shanghai

A Legacy of 21st Century Leadership
A Guide for Creating a Climate of Leadership
Throughout Your Organization

iUniverse books may be ordered through booksellers or by contacting:

iUniverse
2021 Pine Lake Road, Suite 100
Lincoln, NE 68512
www.iuniverse.com
1-800-Authors (1-800-288-4677)

Because of the dynamic nature of the Internet, any Web addresses
or links contained in this book may have changed
since publication and may no longer be valid.

The views expressed in this work are solely those of the author and do not necessarily
reflect the views of the publisher, and the publisher hereby disclaims any responsibility
for them.

ISBN: 978-0-595-44204-1 (pbk)
ISBN: 978-0-595-68802-9 (cloth)
ISBN: 978-0-595-88535-0 (ebk)

Printed in the United States of America

There may be "born leaders," but there surely are far too few of them to depend on them. Leadership must be learned and can be learned.
—Peter F. Drucker

We are made wise, not by the recollection of our past, but by the responsibility for our future.
—Bernard Shaw

The future we predict today is not inevitable. We can influence it, if we know what we want it to be.
—Charles Handy

Contents

Preface

Our greatest responsibility is to be good ancestors.

Jonas Salk

Many thought leaders and authors have gone before us on the legacy theme. Recent works have addressed legacy from life story, spiritual, and organizational points of view (Spence 1997; Meyer 2002; Brooks et al. 2004; Kouzes and Posner 2006), all of which are worthy sight lines for individual reflection and goal setting. Even *Claiming Your Place at the Fire*, Leider and Shapiro's (2004) very fine bestseller on living the last half of your life with purpose, poses profound thoughts for us to ponder about the specific legacy we have left to give in our final decades. It turns out it's plenty.

Our approach comes from a slightly different point of origin, with a slightly different context. We approach legacy through the prism of leadership and leadership through the prism of learning. This line of sight to legacy emanates from our career work in leadership development in the military, universities, private sector, government, and international sectors, where we have been privileged to serve thousands of learners by facilitating discovery of lessons on leadership. We acknowledge researcher and author Marcus Buckingham's caution that corporate America has overcomplicated the role of leader. We will try to be pithy rather than verbose. You will come to learn that we don't believe you have to master all the elements of leadership we write about. We believe it is possible to uncomplicate leadership by focusing on fundamental and meaningful outcomes (legacy), accelerating leadership strengths (rather than laboring away on weaknesses), and carefully considering your strategies for creating a leadership climate.

Elements of what we identify as twenty-first century leadership were indeed percolating earlier in the literature than December 31, 1999. Most certainly Peter Drucker's early writing on management (1967), Donald Schon's seminal work on "learning societies" and learning organizations (1973), Warren Bennis and Burt Nanus's discourse on a search for new leadership (1985), Tom Peter's challenge to thrive on chaos (1987), Ed Oakley and Doug Krug's characterization of "enlightened leadership," (1991) Charles Handy's reflection on "discontinuous change" (1990), and Peter Senge's perspectives on leading learning organizations (1990) all predated the turn of this century by many years. Yet today, it's possible to discern a set of challenges and principles that, to us, clearly converge to suggest what twenty-first century leadership should look like.

We do believe twenty-first century leadership is different; however, we don't intend to suggest great leaders across history haven't demonstrated the approaches we write about. It is not our purpose to claim rights to the topics of leadership and legacy, nor is it our intent to pronounce our perspective any better than others who have written eloquently on the topic. It is our purpose to suggest that the demands on organizational leadership have shifted significantly in the last couple of decades and great leaders keep recalibrating their talent and strategy. It is our purpose to challenge the reader with several fundamental thoughts, one of which is that you're leaving a legacy whether you're thinking about it or not. We believe that thinking about legacy and making your legacy intentional are most likely to strengthen much-needed leadership in today's organizational life, wherever you may live it.

We also challenge the reader to think differently about leadership. Being an excellent manager is not being a great leader. We find too many people confusing their managerial success with leadership success. We find too many organizations believing leadership only really starts when a manager reaches the top third of the corporate hierarchy. We find far too many people calling themselves leaders while only actually executing old-school managerial responses to today's organizational issues.

Finally, in this work we will limit our focus to those who lead in organizational life and the leadership challenges therein, rather than leaders of social or political movements. To that end, we do take encouragement from a young boy from South Africa whose story you might have missed but whose message we believe is worth taking to heart as a legacy wake-up call for us all. While it occurred within a social and political context, we can powerfully generalize it for all leadership situations.

Xolani Nkosi Johnson (1989–2001), of South Africa, was born HIV positive and orphaned at an early age. "Nkosi," as he came to be known, was adopted by a local single woman who nurtured and encouraged his life. When it was time for school, Nkosi was denied admission because of his illness and so began an individual advocacy campaign for the rights of ill children to access education in his homeland. His advocacy became an international movement. Nkosi (his name, in Zulu, means Lord or King of Kings) died at age twelve, but not before he had challenged the world with a determined and profound speech at the 2000 International AIDS Conference in South Africa (Nkosi 2000). Throughout his short life, Nkosi reminded us, with passion and courage, to ponder our legacies.

He frequently paraphrased eighteenth-century theologian John Wesley (Wooten 2004):

> Do all that you can.
> With what you have.
> In the time that you have.
> In the place you are.
>
>   Nkosi

It is from this young man's simple platform that we ask you to begin a reflective journey around leadership, learning, and legacy in your twenty-first century organization.

Introduction: A Legacy Perspective

**Legacy: something handed down from an
ancestor or predecessor or from the past**

Effective leaders make a difference, and they leave legacies. People remember their leaders: how they made them feel, positive changes they shepherded, or capabilities they helped develop in others. Whether you assume a leadership role in a crisis situation or serve as a leader in an organization for an extended period of time, you leave behind an imprint of your leadership. Some imprints are healthy, some less so. Simply remember the climate of leadership and performance you may have inherited throughout your career to validate our case.

We have all heard about leaving legacies, most recently in the context of how politicians try to "manage" their own legacies while in office, or even after they depart, so that everyone has fond memories of them. That being the case, can a politician, or any leader for that matter, "manage" his or her own legacy?

Many have attempted to answer that question and in the last decade, research emanating from case studies, surveys, focus groups, and twenty-first century leadership theory share a common finding: *effective leaders never stop learning*. That is, they never reach the final destination in their leadership journey. They continue learning, adapting, and seeking impact as they come into contact with new people, organizations, opportunities, and dilemmas. While core values may remain steadfast and their leadership competencies may mature, great leaders seek ongoing opportunities to enhance their own leadership impact and the imprint they leave on an organization—legacy. While some imprints share common attributes, an individual leader's impact can vary from organization to organization or from lower to higher leadership levels within an organization. Organizations and/or specific workgroups may have different needs and challenges that require a leader to focus their attention on particular values and competencies. A leader may leave a legacy of integrity, transparency, and a commitment to learning in one situation and may find different priorities in another. In fact, great leaders know that a "textbook" approach to leadership will not yield the kind of legacy they seek not only with the people they lead, but also with the organizations they serve.

With all this ambiguity concerning leadership and leaving a positive legacy, how does a leader approach this difficult task? To explore the landscape of potential legacies, a leader might begin by focusing on some recognized best-practice leadership competencies (e.g., leading change, collaboration, leveraging diversity, and developing others). Numerous researchers have closely examined today's most successful organizations and leaders and have suggested a list of common competencies possessed by the best. Typically, the research identifies a core of ten to twenty competencies and/or characteristics that differentiate great leaders and organizations from the rest (Zenger and Folkman 2002). We've even supplied a list from which we lead leadership discussions (Appendix 1). Supposedly, if a leader focuses his or her attention on some or all of these items, he or she can move from good to great and can ensure that he or she leaves a positive legacy. However, from most of this competency research, a leader may gain very little insight into which of these characteristics and/or competencies is more important than the others and may wonder where to start on this daunting challenge. Does your organization require ongoing transformation and flexibility right now or should you focus more on developing others or on embedding a new era of collaboration in the organizational culture? The point is that great leaders learn the solutions to these leadership dilemmas day-to-day in organizations worldwide. The key resides in the learning process and not necessarily in the competencies and characteristics themselves.

Recently, we heard a leadership lecturer proclaim that leadership has not changed since biblical times. While we realize that certain leadership values and virtues have remained constant over time (e.g., integrity, service, power of vision), we also believe that one of the very few enduring characteristics of great leaders, of earlier eras or more recent, is their capacity for ongoing learning. To say that none of us have learned anything new about leadership in over two thousand years might imply that all leaders can become unthinking automatons following the same basic leadership "textbook" approach in all situations. Indeed, the last two decades of research and teaching have provided valuable clarity as to how leadership is learned and therefore, how to help you and others learn to become better leaders. *Fortune* magazine even went so far as to lead their story on "What it Takes to Be Great" by announcing: "Research now shows that the lack of natural talent is irrelevant to great success. The secret? Painful and demanding practice and hard work" (*Fortune* 30 October 2006). We're not certain that talent is irrelevant, but the point about learning is crucial to effective leadership and leadership development.

We think of leadership as a portfolio of characteristics and competencies that we grow over time as we learn to deal with varying situations and circumstances.

Thus, a growing portfolio helps determine a leader's legacy as does the business situations in which they find themselves. Yes, talent does help differentiate some leaders from others; however, great leaders know that when they stop learning, they stop leading. *Grow your leadership portfolio and your legacy will come into sharper focus.*

Twenty-first Century Leadership

As a means of establishing our bearings in the leadership legacy landscape, we begin this book in Chapter I by examining some dichotomies we have observed over the years representing a significant change from the leadership of the distant and not so distant past. We present these dichotomies as opportunities for learning as a leader and as a means of growing a leadership portfolio and not necessarily as either/or choices. In some cases, leaders might find that a both/and approach to some of these dichotomies is a better choice. In fact, most leaders become quite frustrated with either/or choices and often seek to apply the best combination of both choices for the situation and move forward. We believe that great leaders learn this characteristic and that the process of learning is just as, if not more, important than the decision itself.

We intend to be a bit provocative and certainly recognize that the ten elements in this chapter do not fully define the twenty-first century landscape. However, we believe if you've been paying attention, you will find that we have captured opportunities for huge impact facing you right where you are at this moment.

Commitment to Leadership

Chapter II explores some important lessons we've learned over the years from leaders who have chosen to lead. Leading in today's environment requires a personal decision to act stemming from understanding your own beliefs about why leadership is important. Twenty-first century leadership is not about the pay, the power and control over others, nor the opportunity to bask in the limelight. These beliefs only create a false, externally driven leadership identity that alienates you from others and possibly from your true self as well. Ultimately, leadership is an act of faith in others. If you do not understand your own beliefs, it becomes difficult to believe in others. Great leaders understand why they lead and let go of their desire to control people and organizations through positional power or the force of their personalities. They tear down these barriers, fight the conformity of highly structured organizational cultures, and develop deep relationships with those they serve. Their total commitment moves other people to commitment. We present several ideas about how we see twenty-first century leadership so that you can reflect upon your beliefs and make your own choice and commitment to lead. Indeed, you have to figure out for yourself why you lead. When you find your own absolutely original answer, it comes from what you've learned, it's lastingly satisfying, it leads to spectacular results, and it ensures your leadership legacy.

High-Performance Leadership

In Chapter III, we suggest the many ways in which leadership drives high-performance cultures. Transformational leaders set the context and attitude for their organizations and create an environment where a passion for high performance and energy for excellence thrives. They don't use hope as their strategy to positively shape their organization's culture. They clearly understand that they can exert a very powerful influence on culture if they choose to—but it's hard work! Savvy leaders don't assume or guess at the necessary structural components of a high-performance leadership culture. They participate in the culture and norms of the organization and they understand how to apply the necessary levers to allow a high-performance leadership culture to pervade the organization. In fact, transformational leaders often choose culture as the legacy or imprint on the organization that they will pass on to their successor.

The Legacy Triad

We present these three concepts as the main constructs of a leadership legacy. We believe a leader's legacy emerges from the confluence of learned twenty-first century leadership principles, an evident commitment to lead, and leading a high-performance environment. Figure 1 graphically depicts this view of how you might consider your impact upon leadership legacy.

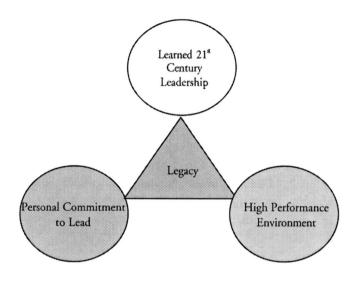

Leadership Legacy Lessons from the Research

One-on-one executive coaching experiences often focus on helping leaders be aware of and take responsibility for the effects of their actions on others. Leadership development often focuses on discovering one's weaknesses and building development plans around them. Over time, the organizational research has matured in its ability to sort out and focus leadership capabilities that make significant impacts upon organizational success and how best to coach and develop them. There may be some surprises here.

Chapter IV takes a look at the leadership competency literature and some specific live assessment data from organizations and their leaders. We confront a few age-old assumptions about leadership development, share some applied research of our own, and link the conclusions to research being conducted by other organizations. We believe the conclusions are instructive for those leaders looking to focus their learning and, in turn, focus their legacies. We know that a legacy, or any business result for that matter, cannot be accomplished by trying to be all things to all people. In this section, we dare to generalize from our research to help you zero in on your own development and the development of others. What might be the vital few elements of your leadership impact? What might be the vital few developmental approaches to enhance the ability of others to also make a leadership impact?

A Legacy Important to Where You Are

Great leaders take time for inner exploration and ask continually what their purpose in life might be, what they want to accomplish, and what they want to leave as their legacy. In this section of the book, we ask you to reflect on the leadership legacy that may be important for where you now lead. Because you are leaving a leadership legacy—ready or not—we encourage you to make it intentional and focused—intentional in that you strategically recognize and choose the leadership behaviors that will make the most difference and focused, in that you clearly see the needed outcome and passionately stay the course to deliver the impact needed by your organization. Take some time with the reflective questions as a means of getting a better grip on your critical leadership impact. Reflection is not soft work. Leadership impact in the moment of action is significantly enhanced by the commitment to ongoing contemplation about leadership. It's the hard work that leaders commit to in order to learn and enhance their success.

Ensuring a Leadership Legacy Strategy

As the leadership legacy you wish to leave comes into focus, in Chapter VI we ask you to consider the strategic behaviors and actions that will ensure the outcome you desire. What might be the primary channels through which a climate of leadership and your legacy take root? What specific actions must you take and what actions must you facilitate in others to endow your legacy?

While the list of strategies may be endless and certainly situational to the culture within which you lead, we suggest ten common strategies that have big impact. They won't all pertain to your situation, but we believe you will certainly see yourself in the reflective questions they bring to bear on your efforts. We believe these ten will cause you to identify other strategies that may also be important to where you lead. Treat them as catalysts rather than limited laws of organizational behavior.

Ten Legacies Worthy of the Twenty-first Century

We admit to being provocative with some of our thoughts and suggestions. Our intent is to stretch your thinking, encourage self-reflection, and help you gain clearer leadership focus. In this chapter, we highlight ten legacies that we believe are at the top of the list of twenty-first century leadership values and legacies to inculcate in organizational behavior. We're not asking for agreement, but rather only for reflection pertaining to your own setting.

Leading Change by Changing the Conversation

In an era of ongoing transformation, leaders certainly recognize that organizational flexibility/adaptability is crucial to survive and thrive. What leaders must accept is their role in helping others gain change compatibility. It's one thing to be personally adaptable, it's quite another to create a climate of leadership where everyone relishes change, has competencies to lead it, and sees value not only in evolution, but also frequent revolution. Chapter VIII asks you to consider how you're leading change and teaching change compatibility. Teaching people to better anticipate change, recover from stumbles, and adapt smoothly to new demands are worthy legacies for the twenty-first century. The late Peter Drucker encouraged us several years ago to make the entire organization a change agent, not simply a few leaders at the top (Drucker 2001). His advice seems even more appropriate today and is a legacy worthy of the twenty-first century.

Lead from Where You Are

In Chapter IX, we speak to multiple leadership situations in which you may find yourself. We briefly suggest some initial thoughts to guide your thinking, whether you're seeking to become a new manager, working for an old school manager but desiring to lead in a twenty-first century manner, or facing serious organizational challenges. Our premise is that whatever your situation, it provides you the opportunity to grow, to reach out to others, and to contribute to a climate of greater leadership right where you are. Leaders remain resolute in climates of the good, the bad, and the ugly, and we offer some of our own thoughts on how you might face those opportunities.

Appendices

"Leadership Succession"

Because of the current panic setting in and among organizations tallying the baby boomers about to retire, we offer our own perspective on succession management—and it is not succession management, it's "leadership succession." Leaders must see their job as developing others and herein resides the solution to the succession management panic.

A Legacy Perspective

We believe our work will be easy reading. We know there won't be total agreement with all of our perspectives. It is to that end that we ask you to challenge assumptions about your leadership and developing other leaders. We don't expect our thoughts on legacy and leadership impact to become yours. We do expect that as a leader you will give thoughtful consideration to the day-to-day impact you have on those around you—family, work associates, and community. If even one thought energizes your commitment, focus, and learning journey, we will consider your investment worthwhile.

A Leadership Legacy Story

Ed, a new executive, had recently taken over an information technology division within a very large financial services organization. His division of about five hundred people managed one of only two nationwide computing centers, which hosted about half of the organization's website and data storage capacity. The division had a long-standing reputation for excessive computer downtime, low productivity, and generally poor customer service, and there were rumors that the organization had made a decision to close the center and consolidate computing capacity at the other location. After about six months on the job getting his bearings, Ed faced the choice of recommending closure or implementing a plan to reenergize the organization, vastly improve the division's performance, and change the division's reputation. While many might have chosen the former path that offered a safer political option, Ed chose the latter because he instinctively knew that his people could flourish under improved leadership. That, he determined, would be his legacy.

Now came the issue that many of us face—how does one increase both leadership effectiveness and employee performance in minimal time so that others can quickly perceive the improvement? A tall order, to be sure, when considering that, like most of us, Ed could not afford an extensive leadership development effort within the meager resources of his reduced budget. Still, he knew that great leaders make a great difference in any type of organization and that he did not have enough great ones among his thirty existing managers. He needed to develop more great leaders or face closure of the center and a layoff of its employees. The challenge was to determine the critical characteristics or competencies for focus and what type of cost-effective developmental effort would achieve more than just incremental improvement. From his own assessment of the division, Ed thought that an emphasis on improving leadership skills involving strategic thinking and adaptability would help him meet his objectives and, at the same time, best achieve the organization's mission. His best decision was to supplement his own instincts about his organization's developmental needs by asking each of his managers to undertake a 360-degree feedback survey. From his own experience, he had learned that such feedback provided valuable insights into improving individual leadership in an organizational context. Fortunately, his agency had designed a customized 360-degree feedback instrument that directly evaluated behaviors associated with the organization's fundamental leadership competencies.

The data gleaned from these assessments yielded tremendous information regarding both managerial performance and developmental needs. Aggregate data from all of the feedback surveys revealed that development focused on technical credibility and developing others offered the best potential for improving overall leadership in his division. This, combined with a customized development plan for each individual manager, meant that with only a small improvement in certain areas, he believed he could achieve breakthrough improvements in both overall leadership effectiveness and employee productivity.

With the data in hand and a clear focus, Ed began a series of one-on-one developmental conversations with those reporting directly to him to begin plans to enhance their leadership capabilities. He created a template for similar discussions that would cascade down through each management level. He obtained help from internal consultants to suggest sources of reading, online learning, and course work for his leaders to access in their developmental journey. Ed also identified a coalition of four of his best managers to be mentors. He chose those capable and willing to teach others and closest to demonstrating the leadership he believed the organization needed to make the next step.

By changing the conversation about leadership focus and creating a learning environment with mentored support, Ed changed the climate of leadership. He saw his job and that of his mentor team was not to solve problems but to teach others to identify the most important issues and find solutions together with their teams. To be sure, this was not an overnight success. Leading a culture change or realignment of leadership focus is a journey. Ed ensured that a climate of learning was established where each manager could safely talk about his or her own learning ups and downs. He ensured that sufficient positive reinforcement accompanied the efforts, and when the organizational metrics began to shift in a positive direction, he made sure that the information was transparent and celebrated as short-term wins indicative of progress.

Ed's focus on the climate of leadership was not without other tough choices. Three managers opted out of management. Two others had to be replaced. While giving everyone a supportive focus for leadership development, he was also forced to deal with those who chose not to go on the journey and with those who were in the wrong place for the type of leadership Ed expected.

Certainly, Ed's approach did not show dividends right away. While it is possible to manage some short-term outcomes to demonstrate turnaround, Ed chose a more comprehensive strategy: change the culture of leadership. This was certainly risky in a period of poorer organizational performance and greater expectations from higher ups that Ed would produce immediate results. Ed discovered what the research on adoption of change (Rogers 2003) would generally tell us. About 15 percent of his leadership cadre were ready for a different conversation about leading the organization and took to the development program with energy and immediate impact. The next 30 percent quickly clamored aboard the initiative when they saw opinion leaders weighing in, and key indicators showing initial positive movement, they also noticed that Ed was not simply trying another quick fix that would lose support in a few months.

Within months, Ed reached a tipping point of leadership energy. Organizational associates saw the conversations on strategic thinking bring out business environment conditions of which they were less aware, felt drawn to the opportunities for being more successful, and valued their opportunity to weigh in on where the organization was and where it might need to go. Slowly at first, and then with more momentum, organizational associates began surfacing new ideas, challenging old assumptions, and believing that including customers in their future planning was a helpful idea.

At the five-month milestone, people began seeing positive indicators of improvement and felt a momentum about the new strategic and inclusive atmosphere. By eight months, kudos were coming from headquarters about the turnaround and at fourteen months, it was clear the performance improvement was sustainable and not simply a quick-fix initiative. Ed was then selected for another headquarters position overseeing research and development and his successor was promoted from within. What remained the same despite the personnel changeover was the embedded learning behavior that Ed created: think strategically, bolster technical competence, coach and grow leadership capabilities at all levels, and be inclusive in signing up everyone to lead.

Three years later, Ed's information technology division continues to be known for spinning off great leaders for elsewhere in the organization and for sustainable breakthrough performance, a sure sign that Ed's effort grew roots and embedded itself within the culture—a legacy.

In Ed's new assignment in R & D, he's brought a leadership approach of developing products and services in the lap of the customer—a new legacy. And he continues his focus on developing others. Most organizations adopt a slogan similar to "Our people are our most important resource." Ed's take on this is different; he maintains, "Our work is our most important resource to develop our people." That is the type of different thinking that we think is both indicative and required of great twenty-first century leaders.

▼

CHAPTER I

A TWENTY-FIRST CENTURY LEADERSHIP PERSPECTIVE

The days of the heroic or great leader taking up space in the room—air, spotlight, and vision included—are over."

Andre Martin

Whereas the heroic manager of the past knew all, could do all, and could solve every problem, the post-heroic manager asks how every problem can be solved in a way that develops other people's capacity to handle it.

Charles Handy

The age of heroic leadership is over. The myth of the "great man" or "great woman" leading larger than life rescuing powerless organizational associates has been dispelled. Great leadership occurs in a "culture of leadership" which is expected, developed, and distributed at all levels of the organization where people can display their natural ability to learn, adapt, and yes, lead.

1. **Transform Rather than Rescue:** While it is true that periodic exigencies hit the desks of leaders, *today's leadership is more about ongoing transformation than seasonal rescue.* And maybe it's more about revolution than evolution. Not only is the world more chaotic and complex, but also the velocity of growing complexity is accelerating. Donald Sull of the London Business School captures this intense pressure not only to change reactively but also to transform proactively. He notes, "Uncertain markets exert an unforgiving selection pressure on companies by churning out an unrelenting series of opportunities and threats. New companies emerge to pursue novel opportunities, while established companies that cannot

adapt fail. The only way to avoid this harsh Darwinian pressure is to adapt to changing circumstances before market pressures select against your company" (Sull 2006). In their own way, governments and non-governmental organizations around the globe experience similar pressures.

The pace of growing complexity demands that the twenty-first century organization listen more closely to external trends and business environment shifts, believe in ongoing change, and set the bar high for revolutionizing themselves regularly. Hamel and Valikangas (2003) remind us: "In the past, executives had the luxury of assuming that business models were more or less immortal. Companies always had to work to get better, of course, but they seldom had to get different—not at their core, not in their essence. Today, getting different is the imperative." In *Leading the Revolution*, Gary Hamel is even more passionate about the need for organizational transformation in the twenty-first century by declaring, "Evolution keeps us alive; revolution keeps us relevant" (Hamel 2000).

The status quo is slow death and transformational leaders help people let go of old models that worked in the past for new models that better fit the developing environment. We all become limited by comfort and reliance on established mental models of how enterprises should behave. As numerous authors have pointed out over the last couple of decades, leadership in a post-modern world requires that we challenge traditional mental models (Wind et al. 2004). Leaders tend to be able to create a sense of excitement about where the organization can go rather than a sense of remorse for the models they must leave behind.

Rather than annual "strategy" sessions, twenty-first century leaders *create ongoing conversations about the future, helping the organization think more strategically and challenge assumptions about their models.* These conversations also help the organization make contingency plans by anticipating different scenarios of challenge and success. Regular, last-minute, reactive, heroic rescue is a sign your organization might benefit from greater transformational leadership.

- Where might you still be behaving as a rescuer?
- What are the major challenges/opportunities for transforming your organization/work unit?
- What's the most critical large-scale change that needs to be made to keep your organization relevant and valuable?
- How are you creating ongoing conversations about the future in order to ensure strategic thinking and external awareness? Is this happening throughout the organization or only at the top levels of leadership?

2. **Leveraging Diversity or Just Like Me:** If it's up to the individual leader to create the organizational values and then hold people accountable, there will always be a top-down mantra to them rather than a community of ownership. Yes, leaders stand up for values and model personal responsibility. They even demand that values shift when the internal and external environments require it. But lasting greatness comes from broad ownership rather than the single-minded will of one leader. A great leader is neither an island nor the source of all wisdom.

In today's organization, the diverse backgrounds and perspectives require that organizational values be shaped by leveraging that diversity. Remember, you're dealing with volunteers here. This doesn't mean traditional values of integrity, teamwork, and commitment have to be diluted. It does mean that values of work ethic, valuing diverse input, respecting differences, and relationships with the greater community require a different leadership than in the last century. In *Authentic Leadership*, Bill George talks about this cultural quality as "not a question of achieving affirmative action quotas, but rather of building breadth of thought and opinion into the decision making process" (George 2003). David Thomas and Robin Ely's very fine article on this aspect of diversity reminds us that "diversity should be understood as the varied perspectives and approaches to work that members of different identity groups bring" (Thomas and Ely 1996). *This is more than respecting differences; it is about strategically using differences as an organizational resource for effectiveness.*

- Who can you count on to keep alternative ideas and non-traditional thinking in your line of sight?
- How well does your organization do at respecting and leveraging differences among the team? How well do you model this behavior?
- Is your commitment to diversity of thought reflected in your organization's recruitment and selection process?
- What two people closest to you are also very different than you? Or, do you all seem to think alike?

3. **Distributed Leadership vs. Top Down:** In the movies of the 1950s, the hero was always a bit taller, more brazen, and a better communicator, and he always possessed a magical sense of accuracy with his decisions. The citizens and community leaders always stood behind him as "hero" interfaced with a villain or threat. When a team looks to a single source for rescue or guidance, they're playing a risky game. Twenty-first century leadership requires a different model built upon a phalanx of leaders, all capable, confident, and prepared for the villains and

threats to their organization: leaders at all levels. Yes, employees and staff also step up to leadership.

Where the heroic leader may only see other leaders around them, the transformational leader seeks out, develops, and rewards leadership at all levels. Transformational leaders believe in distributing leadership and can be seen mentoring, coaching, and ensuring development resources are invested in all managers and staff in the organization. The self-confidence based upon competency development, clear objectives, and interdependent collaboration built by transformational leaders permeates the organization. Resiliency and resolve is built deeper into the bench rather than with only a few power hitters. Twenty-first century leadership commits to developing successors so that when one generation of leaders move on, a legacy of leadership is maintained.

- Does the organization depend on only a few "key people" to provide leadership?
- How are you ensuring your management team is distributing and developing leadership from top to bottom?

4. "Our" vs. "My" Vision, Mission, and Values: The age of heroic leadership gave great credit to the dynamic leader bringing his or her personal version of nirvana to the huddled organizational masses. The age of *transformational leadership finds stronger power in the facilitation of a common, energizing, long-term vision owned by architects organization-wide.* Yes, this is more difficult. Yet, we all care for a product we help build and fight for a goal we help set with greater vigilance than one given to us by others. Simon Cooper, President of Ritz Carlton, captured it best when he observed, "No one is more apathetic than in pursuit of someone else's goal" (Cooper 2005). Senge (1990) contrasts the generic "vision statement" so popular in this era with "genuine vision." Genuine vision consists of "pictures of the future" commonly shared across the organization—shared, not because the leader said so, but because people have been involved in shaping this powerful view of their future.

Heroes certainly have that fiery speech and energizing "rah rah" that can send teams into frenzied short-term effort. Transformational leaders, however, imbue a sense of quiet community "can do" and we stay on the bus long term because we all feel ownership. While the big "V" vision may still cascade from above, every function and work unit should have their own version: the little "v" vision created through group effort.

- How broadly have you invited input into organizational vision and values?
- How broadly known is the organizational vision?
- How broadly supported is the organizational vision?
- Does each unit with your organization create a little "v" vision in support of the big "V" overall vision?
- Do you see buy-in, consistency, advocacy, and accountability regarding mission, vision, and values all the way to the frontline? What's your evidence?

5. Critical Thinking vs. Linear, Hierarchical Thinking: "Promise to disagree with me," may be the mantra of the transformational leader. When we all think alike, no one seems to really "think" much. Last century's model of looking to the top for answers or worse yet, following a tried and true multi-layer linear process to reach decisions, fails to keep organizations relevant to rapidly shifting problems, values, and models. A less symmetrical input and thought structure helps create a climate of creativity and critical breakthrough thinking throughout the entire organization. Critical thinking explores challenges from non-traditional as well as traditional perspectives. Transformational leaders forcefully argue against even their own best choices to see if their ideas stand up to close scrutiny. While law enforcement and war strategies are all adapting to "asymmetrical" thinking by our enemies, an organization must also leverage the power of asymmetrical critical thinking. Teaching people to think for themselves in different ways does not mean dismantling organizational authority or values. It does mean twenty-first century leaders recognize that they don't have all the answers and, if they place boundaries on ideas, or require ideas to navigate a thick bureaucratic suggestion box-like maze, they limit their leadership effectiveness.

- How well do you ensure diverse input into organizational thinking and decision making?
- How do you ensure non-traditional ideas are given voice?
- Are major organizational decisions contemplated in an environment of transparency and open source input, or traditional hierarchical process?

6. Dialogue vs. Command and Control: So how do transformational leaders build the capacity and resolve so people accept their own leadership, think critically, and step up when needed? Through ongoing dialogue about how the organization is doing, where it is going, and what might be expected. It is not debate, not discussion, but *true dialogue where value conflicts are uncovered, new opportu-*

nities are discovered, and an informed and strategic perspective is embedded (Yankelovitch 1999). Dialogue applies "both/and" thinking rather than "either/or" thinking. The power of command is great and the dynamism of heroism is electric; however, the perspective, confidence, and capabilities built through transformational leadership live in the organization beyond any heroics. A climate of leadership that values and engages the wisdom of all will discover better answers. Engaging the intellectual capital of your organization requires a commitment to lots of listening, lots of appreciative questioning, and deeper understanding of the motives and perspectives driving your workforce. Twenty-first century leaders find the time to enlarge both the circle of dialogue and investment in real dialogue as a means of keeping fresh, connected, and alert to those they lead.

- How are you ensuring that open communication and quality dialogue are occurring throughout your organization?
- When is the last time you had a quality dialogue (not a command discussion) with constituents closer to the frontline?
- Are your organization's leaders (management team) interpersonally competent or simply command competent?

7. **Ask vs. Tell**: Transformational leaders facilitate mutual success by asking vs. telling. Remember, they look for "both/and" unity rather than "either/or" answers. This requires a patient, facilitative, and interest-based competency. Within a culture of transformational leadership, a greater number of people are better prepared for decisions and problem solving because they are led to explore diverse pathways rather than directed to the easy path. Michael Marquardt has written an entire book on the value of a leader's questions and suggests a "question does more than convey respect for the person to whom it's posed. It actually encourages that person's development as a thinker and problem solver, thereby delivering both the short-term value of generating a solution to the issue at hand and the long-term value of giving subordinates the tools to handle similar issues in the future independently" (Marquardt 2005). In *Funky Business*, the authors encourage leaders to learn to ask questions in unique ways and before others even think of asking (Jonas et al. 2000). In this way, leaders help teach others to always be questioning and therefore help their organization potentially stay ahead of the need for reactive change.

This approach reduces the need for "command" direction. Yes, *even in fairly chaotic emergencies, a team built through transformational leadership will deploy smoothly, adapt more easily, and choose among strategies as a team rather than defer to "the leader."* The marines teach it, the emergency room practices it, and the current U.S. challenge of collaborative intelligence gathering requires it. Organizations built from this type of leadership adapt more quickly and waste less effort than those built upon the leader as hero model.

- How well does your organization make input count?
- Can you identify an organizational change that was made in the last three months based upon input from your frontline employees?
- Does your organization have to rely on suggestion programs to generate fresh and candid thinking or does it emerge from work units organically?
- Do organizational associates believe their opinion counts? How do you know?

8. **Collaboration vs. Cooperation**: Preschoolers are taught to cooperate. Adult success requires collaboration—sharing effort and resources as partners, not simply as good neighbors lending their tools across the fence. In the landscape of transformational leadership, a feeling of "teamness" exists where interdependent collaboration takes place regularly, not simply when the emergency siren sounds. Because "silos" and territoriality occur naturally from the intensive attention to executing tasks at the department and division level, the leader has to work harder to set a standard of collaboration across the enterprise and the value to be derived from our important mission. *Silos need to merge into a cross-functional footprint in all that they do. Functional units need to think in terms of "all of us" rather than just themselves as they make decisions and plans.* Human networks must anticipate the "ripple effects" of their efforts and alert their collaborative partners. Seamless collaborative efforts in planning and execution outperform short rallies of cooperation over the long term.

Territoriality is not only caused by believing your area might be the most important one. Territoriality may also be caused by conflict felt between work units. In their *Harvard Business Review* article, "Want Collaboration?" Weiss and Hughes challenge leaders to focus on the conflicts, not the nice-nice, kumbaya initiatives. "Most companies respond to the challenge of improving collaboration in entirely the wrong way. They focus on the symptoms ('sales and delivery do not work together') rather than on the root cause of failures in cooperation: conflict. The fact is, you can't improve collaboration until you've addressed the issue of conflict" (Weiss and Hughes 2005). Powerful insight we think into diagnosing why you're not getting the interdependency necessary for great outcomes.

- Can you identify the conflict issues hampering collaboration in your organization?
- Do different operating units collaborate seamlessly, without having to be pressured by you?
- Do different operating units solicit input from other units in the course of their planning and decision making?
- Do you have consistent winning outcomes that occurred because departmental silos worked collaboratively?

9. **Passion 24/7 vs. a Job:** The twenty-first century leader believes they are in the job to "do something" rather than having something to do. Heroic passion may well spike to great heights in time of need. However, passionate leadership can also be a choice for steady, resilient, and relentless effort. Passionate leadership can be a commitment to grow others, innovate, and create a quality work life. In *Good to Great*, Jim Collins refers to this type of leadership as "Level 5" leadership. It's neither sensational nor heroic. It is a determined, steady, and humble resolve. Yes, this frequently means leaders suffering and risking for people and causes beyond themselves. Twenty-first century leaders don't decide at the heroic moment to "go," they have decided long ago and demonstrated an unrelenting commitment to new models that keep the organization viable, valuable, and vibrant. In all their messages, they are able to connect the dots between vision, mission, values, and actions.

Life is too short to work in a climate under pressure for which you have no love. We don't have to love everything we do, but we believe an element of twenty-first century leadership is having a passion for leading and helping others find a similar passion. Don't mistake this as 1950s "rah rah." We speak here of valuing what you do and helping others see value for them. While a great speechmaker may rile our emotion on occasion, we refer here to the leader able to use mission connectedness, a common energetic vision, and an appreciation for the contributions of others to build passion.

- Where's the passion in your organization? What does it look like?
- Are your key leaders passionate about the right things?
- Does the entire organization know what your passions are?

10. **Leading** *and* **Following:** It is not an either/or choice. *Transformational leaders know when to lead and when to follow.* If individuals cannot learn to subordinate themselves to a shared purpose, then no one will follow, and selfishness and anarchy may rule. Yet in order to grow and improve, organizations must create a climate that fosters leadership; they must encourage the honest articulation of fresh strategic visions of the future. Leaders need to be forward looking, have a sense of direction, and be concerned about the future of the organization. *Followership means we rely on each other, set aside personal agendas, and collaborate for the good of the organization.* It also means being coachable and accepting the feedback and ideas of others. The tension between leading and following is acute in many organizations clinging to hierarchical leadership. The tension between leading and following is challenging to any organization that has not clearly defined their leadership model and the climate of leadership expected throughout. Where do your associates see you modeling good followership?

- Where do your staff and employees see you displaying willing followership, both internal and external?

- How well does your management team display intelligent choices in when to lead and when to follow?

- What does followership look like in your organization? Is it seen as pejorative or complimentary?

- Where does your organization observe you being coachable—open to candid feedback and the ideas of others?

Transformational Rather Than Transactional

If you've been following the last couple of decades of leadership thought, you may recognize the prior leadership elements as characteristic of transformational leadership as contrasted with transactional leadership. Transactional leadership—most characteristic of what we refer to as twentieth century leadership—revolves around "transactions" between leader and followers based on self-interest and managing and controlling the enterprise. The source of influence in a transactional model is position or command authority. Put in traditional management jargon, it is planning, organizing, coordinating, directing, and controlling. Organizations need these transactional functions adequately fulfilled.

Transformational leadership engages people beyond self-interest based on moving the enterprise to new strategic positions, accomplishments, and innovations. The source of influence is not positional or hierarchical, but expertise, credibility, interpersonal competence, and role modeling. Put in traditional leadership jargon—it is developing others, culture building, strategic thinking, and marked change (transformation).

Another way to conceptualize the differences between transactional and transformation leadership may be to contrast the leadership focus. In Figure 2, we've exaggerated the differences in order to provide the reader a clearer feel for our characterization of transformational or twenty-first century leadership. (In their book, *The High Impact Leader*, Bruce Avolio and Bernard Bass [2002] provide an informative look at transactional and transformational leadership approaches in case studies of twenty-eight leaders.)

Some simple directional differences:

Heroic	Transformational
I	We
I'll handle it	What shall we do?
My vision	Our vision
Boss	Coach
Tell	Ask
Egocentric	Others centric
Independent	Interdependent
Exclusive	Inclusive
Push	Pull
Uses Fear	Uses Confidence
Secretive	Transparent
Takes credit	Gives credit
Business results	Balanced measures
Closed	Open
Limited input	Lots of input
Selfish	Giving
Control	Facilitate
Stability	Change
Either/Or	Both/And
Win/Lose	Win/Win
Operational	Strategic

Figure 2: Transactional vs. Transformational Leadership Focus

By defining twenty-first century leadership, we by no means intend to imply that many of these leadership characteristics were not present or recognized in prior centuries. We only mean to suggest that as we entered the twenty-first century, there is developing clarity about what leadership competencies and focus tend to be best matched for the challenges that abound.

Applied Reflection

Leaders Are Learners: Take a moment and jot down some impressions from reading the prior section that may be relevant to your own leadership perspective and growth.

I might need to think differently about how I …

I might use the following thoughts to better coach other leaders …

Of all the elements mentioned regarding twenty-first century leadership, I seem to be strongest at …

Of all the elements mentioned in this section, it might help to get some advice from others about how I might improve …

CHAPTER 11

▼

CHOOSING TO LEAD

There is a romantic notion that the best leaders do not thrust themselves forward but are sought out. In reality, almost all young leaders nominate themselves—over and over, if necessary.

John Gardner

The day-to-day oversight, direction, and control of management are easier than maintaining the focus, engaged relationships, and forward-thinking risk involved in leadership. But it is your choice! The "will" to lead helps set leaders apart from caretakers. If comfort, routine, and low risk is your style, you may not be ready to lead within the challenges faced by contemporary enterprise. If seeing groups and organizations achieve extraordinary outcomes while helping them lead them-selves is comfortable for you, then choose to lead! *Not one single leadership princi-ple requires permission from anyone other than you.* No excuses, you're not a victim. What are you waiting for?

1. **Leadership Is Not Just about Leading:** It's more about the culture of leadership than about you as a leader. The age of heroic leadership is over. Great leadership occurs in a "climate of leadership" which is expected, developed, and distributed at all levels of the organization. If it's still about "you" in your organization, you're missing the point. If leaders in your organization are still trying to be the "great man" or "great woman" leading larger-than-life, you missed the millennial turn. How many people have you encouraged to lead this week? Who are you developing?

- How does your team describe the climate of leadership that you've facilitated?

- How much are you having to direct vs. how much does the entire team step up to leadership?

13

2. Leadership Is about Adaptability: "Constant change" is readily recognized as the norm in organizational life. Over a decade ago, Peter Vaill labeled this challenge "permanent white water," playing on the metaphor of navigating a river in constant turbulence (Vaill 1996). That's why "adaptability," "flexibility," "change compatibility," or some combinations thereof frequently show up on corporate leadership competency sets. If twenty-first century leadership is about transformation and morphing strategy to the ever-changing challenges, then a climate of leadership flexibility is critical.

A commitment to leadership adaptability means not only flexible leadership, but it also means creating that same change compatibility in the organizational culture. Leaders constantly give voice to changing business conditions, encourage vision over the horizon, and provide migration strategies that help all of us change with as much dignity and as little pain as possible.

Twenty-first century challenges suggest that ongoing transformation of the enterprise is one of the biggest challenges of leadership. The late Peter Drucker encouraged that *the "enterprise has to become a change agent" rather than relying on periodic heroic moves by top management to forge transition"* (Drucker 2001). The status quo is slow death; help your organization live. Be strategically proactive, not reactive.

- Can the average organizational associate articulate the reasons why the organization must be constantly changing and the vision toward which you journey?
- Is change mostly initiated from the top down or do leadership associates at all levels identify opportunities and energize change?
- Is the organization change compatible enough to flex with ease vs. brittle and vulnerable to setbacks when change must occur?

3. Leadership Is about Relationships: A climate of leadership occurs when people stretch their thinking and offer their discretionary effort beyond the job description. To get that added value, the leader must care about how others are doing, be interested in their work lives, and be highly visible to their efforts. *Let people see the person behind the position, give trust to get trust, and demonstrate sincere interest in helping people be more successful.* Fiery team speeches, hard-nosed pressure, and wielding the ax are old hat. Clarity of focus, interdependency between operations, and commitment throughout evolves from the relationships you build.

Relationships and the trust required for twenty-first century leadership don't happen by spontaneous combustion—this is hard work requiring a commitment and resolve to know yourself and care enough to know others. Daniel Goleman (1995) captured the significance of this commitment when he confirmed the research about leaders developing "emotional intelligence." Leaders knowing themselves well enough to be socially and interpersonally adept at building powerfully successful relationships tend to outperform others in any professional setting. Although we all felt we knew this, Goleman brings clarity to the puzzle of self-mastery and social mastery. Margaret Wheatley also makes a strong case for leaders investing in "relationship authenticity" in her powerful essay grounding a leader's ability to cope with the overwhelming chaos and change of the twenty-first century directly to the strength of relationships they have built across their organization (Effron et al. 2003).

Leadership, after all, is neither a position nor a role in the organization. In our interactions with individual employees, teams, groups, and organizations, we often ask them to describe great leadership. A frequent response is: "I know it when I see it." Probing deeper, we discover that the primary source of this sentiment stems from a sense that those employees truly know that leader considers their success at least as important as, if not more important than, his or her own success. As a result, we believe that leadership is a relationship among a group of individuals seeking the synchronicity of individual and enterprise success.

- What does your 360-degree feedback tell you about your relationships?
- What does your organization's climate assessment tell you about how well distributed a relationship focus is?
- Can you cite specific instances where you've outwardly displayed the sense that you consider your employees' success more important than your own success? Would they agree?

4. **Focus on the Vital Few**: Having an overly ambitious, busy set of priorities is the most common mistake made by inexperienced folks attempting leadership. Interestingly, business schools have perpetuated the notion that we all need to use our intelligence, drive, creativity, and innovation to analyze situations and create solutions to the myriad problems that exist in organizations. So, being true to that model, we initiate numerous projects, create action-oriented teams, and generally try to resolve every issue. At times, the standard of success revolves around how "busy" we are and we usually deliver on that objective in spades! Some managers might actually create problems where none exist in order to continue to look busy. As a result, the average leader simultaneously juggles countless "balls"

in the air, tirelessly toils all day and into the night, and arrives home exhausted from the daily grind.

In the twenty-first century, we don't necessarily consider the best leaders as those who work the hardest, but as those who actually finish something important! They achieve results that are enormously critical to the organization. They realize that they must invest the limited time and energy they have on the most important issues. *They work with other leaders in the organization to whittle down a long list of priorities and initiatives to a "vital few" which will return the most on their investment effort.* Heroes, or worse yet, heavy-handed senior managers mistaking micro-management with leadership, end up holding back rather than accelerating accomplishment by trying to do it all. The old 80/20 rule is sufficient guidance here: what 20 percent of the priorities will most likely make up to 80 percent of the impact you seek? Focus on those. Give up on some, scale back energy on others, and surround your key objectives with high energy and a massive focus of resources. A "stop doing" list is as important as a long "to do" list!

- Envision the vital few priorities for this quarter: how well can your organizational associates articulate them?

- What have you recently scaled back or rescheduled for later in order to bring an energetic focus to the vital few?

- What do your other organizational leaders believe is something you should stop doing or start doing? How often do you have these conversations?

5. **Develop Others**: Recent research suggests efforts to *develop others pay some of the highest return on investment over other leadership competencies* (see Chapter IV). This is a "differentiating" competency with a positive ripple effect on other key leadership competencies such as strategic thinking, problem solving, building relationships, and leading change. Not only does the leader grow in all these areas, but the appreciative support of helping others grow also contributes to a distributed sense of leadership at all levels. Now for the bad news: *too many of us are still acting indispensable and trying to do it all ourselves without teaching others what we know.* How much time are you personally devoting to developing others by giving them challenging assignments and coaching them through? What expectations have you set for making this an enterprise-wide effort?

- Does each person directly reporting to you have a robust leadership (not management) development plan? How often do you have conversations with them about it?

- Is there a robust learning climate in your organization? How do you facilitate it? What would your associates say about your commitment to leadership development?

6. **Connect the Dots**: The story of the stonemason who saw his work as building a cathedral rather than laying stone says it all here. In a climate of leadership, organizational associates believe in the larger importance of their work and feel connected to a common energizing vision of where they are helping to take their organization. Mission connectedness is well known to help people deal with the stress and challenge of transition and problem solving. *The leader's voice ensures that all aspects of the enterprise can connect the dots from their work through the key strategies to the vital mission and vision.* Leaders need to say, "This is where we're going and this is why we need you to get there." Transformational leaders also ensure organizational associates can connect the dots between work, organizational success, and their own personal development.

- What recent conversations can you recall where you talked about the line of sight from an associate's tasks and efforts directly to the organizational strategy and vision?

7. **Execution/Performance Clarity**: Management is not a dirty word, although one might derive that conclusion based on the volume of work being published about leadership and the need for more leadership. Leadership Guru Warren Bennis himself has declared business to be "over managed and under led" (Bennis 2003). Yet, creating the climate of leadership we write about also requires that an enterprise execute its commitments and change initiatives if it is to harvest the bounty that leadership planting and nurturing creates. It's not either/or, leadership or management. "Everything that every effective manager does is sandwiched between action on the ground and reflection in the abstract. Action without reflection is thoughtless; reflections without action is passive" (Gosling and Mintzberg 2003).

We know that successful execution is not a simple formula. However, there are some critical pressure points if successful execution is to be accomplished. Clarity about the what and why are crucial. Most of your associates wish to be successful and a huge contributor to success is clarity of expectations. Most of your associates want to feel they make a difference in the organization's accomplishments and feel deputized when you take the time to explain the "why" behind a direction and an execution process. Understanding the rationale behind anything we are asked to do engages our brain to better problem solve dilemmas as they occur and to offer better execution ideas as we see them. Successful execution also requires transparent feedback about how we're doing—the good, so we can feel appreciation and pride; the bad, so we can troubleshoot in a timely fashion; and the ugly, so we can put our heads together to prevent disaster.

It's also at the execution level where heavy-handed management may enter your leadership climate, uninvited but naturally occurring just the same. Managers who believe that success is measured by delivering at any cost may charge that cost to the workforce in the currency of authoritarian management. The commitment to tactical execution we write about here is characterized by valuing and respecting people and believing the leader's/manager's most important job is to help them be successful with the organizational deliverables they have contracted to deliver. There should be a heavy focus on delivery, yes, but no heavy-handedness.

- Do you balance action and reflection when you focus on execution?
- Do you clearly clarify your expectations (outcomes, not process) to your employees?
- Do you connect the dots for your people between the work they do and the organization's mission?
- How do you help your team get timely feedback during the execution phase?

8. **Integrity**: We could have started here because it all begins and ends with integrity. Many people think they have it and most do. However, *the leadership we write about here is beyond reproach*. Taking an organization to higher performance can be done through lots of approaches, many of which are not leadership and lack integrity. *Short-term selfishness, spikes in performance coming from inflicting pain on people, or prestidigitation with performance measures is not leadership*. In a climate of leadership, values are vivid and there is zero tolerance for anything less than total integrity. People work best when they can believe what they are told. They must know you will back up your commitments and that they do not have to cut corners to be successful. Most of your team can sense integrity and will model your lead. Are you beyond reproach?

- Are you known for zero tolerance around integrity?
- Are the expectations so clear that a frontline associate can recite the organization's commitments?

- Are matters of challenged integrity safely and easily brought to light?
- What most recent "right choice" regarding integrity can you identify that the organization celebrated?
- Are the leaders that you have a hand in selecting recognized for their integrity?

9. **Resiliency/Recovery**: Detours, barriers, lack of cooperation, risk, and sudden shifts in the environment derail the average person from forging ahead with their dreams. Leaders provide a realistic "can do" support to critical success objectives by removing barriers, encouraging people to stay the course, and giving permission for risk taking. This doesn't mean a Pollyanna view of challenges. It does mean *leaders never see themselves as victims and rarely take no for an answer.* They are adept at energizing people to see pathways that get to goals despite challenging conditions. Most people are fairly resilient and creative when given permission. What chronic outcome measures or performance challenges continue to resist improvement? That's where "make it happen" leadership can be the most helpful. *Any fool can throw money at a problem; leaders energize the human spirit to go for it and help navigate the narrows when needed.*

Much of life is recovering from missteps or the challenges provided by trying to live happy and healthy. Leaders understand this and don't take setback as failure. *True leaders don't refer to, or see, failure. Instead, they recognize that not all outcomes will be optimal and some may even be disastrous at first, but they are only failures if we give up or fail to learn.* Getting up, dusting yourself off, and re-engaging the challenge is what leadership is all about. Life may be a series of recoveries and so is leadership. Learn, adapt, change directions, and go again. But fail? Not in our vocabulary.

- What have been your most satisfying impacts on helping your associates "make it happen" despite heavy odds or misfortune?
- What chronic challenge might benefit from your "make it happen" leadership?
- How have you helped your organization recover from less than optimal outcomes? Was your success based upon rescue or transformational leadership?
- What were the leadership lessons available in doing no-fault post mortems of less than optimal outcomes?

10. **Balance and an Enjoyable Work Environment**: Balance, personal development, celebration, appreciation, and enjoying the job are all noted in the contemporary organizational literature as challenges of the twenty-first century workplace. An entire field of study and endeavor has grown up around quality of work life and the cultures of preferred employers. Tension, stress, and frustration make up many daily work environments and it's much more pronounced in some industries than others. Leaders must work harder to ensure that there is fun, optimism, and creativity in the culture to buffer the daily breeches of civility and setback felt by associates. Relationships need to be friendly and collaborative; internal systems need to ensure they don't add more fear or frustration. *The transformational leader presses the culture to not become another obstacle in the work of staff but to be a smooth, supportive safe harbor where people can go about a tough job in a nurturing environment.* Also, please leave your family a legacy—one where professional accomplishment is balanced with a rich personal life.

- How well do you model navigating the challenging balance between life and work?
- What support do your organizational associates see from you in their efforts to navigate a reasonable balance of life and work?
- Is there leadership opportunity to influence organizational values and policy toward being a preferred employer known for your life/work philosophy?

Applied Reflection

Leaders Are Learners: Take a moment and jot down some impressions from reading the prior section that may be relevant to your own leadership perspective and growth.

I might need to think differently about how committed I am to ...

I might use the following thoughts to better coach other leaders ...

Of all the elements mentioned regarding choosing to lead, I seem to be strongest at ...

Of all the elements mentioned in this section, it might help to get some advice from others about how I might improve ...

CHAPTER III

▼

HIGH-PERFORMANCE LEADERSHIP CULTURES

We are what we repeatedly do; excellence, then, is not an act, but a habit.

Aristotle

Organizational culture, written about extensively in the academic literature of the 1980s, has almost gained cult status as a target of definition, measurement, criticism, and change focus. In its simplest form, organizational culture refers to the values, beliefs, and behaviors demonstrated by the organization, its leaders, and staff. Culture characteristics can range from entrepreneurial to bureaucratic, innovative to risk averse, or customer-centric to cost-centric. Weak cultures are characterized in the research literature as ones having to use control and pressure to force associates to align with their expectations. Strong cultures are characterized by associates who behave in strong alignment to organizational values. In the leadership literature, culture is deemed as one of the most difficult aspects of an organization or work unit to change. It is also one of the few things in an organization upon which a leader can exert the most influence. Whatever you believe the culture of your organization to be, we provide below a summary of what many contemporary views of leadership and organizational culture would consider characteristics of a high-performance leadership culture.

In a high-performance culture, the organization consistently retains and grows value (i.e., stockholder, citizen, and customer), remains vibrant even in the face of downturn and dramatic shifts in the business environment, and sustains viability (relevance) even while traversing challenging conditions. We believe the following are important pressure points to ensuring a high-performance culture.

1. Dialogue: "Communication" is much too abstract a word to effectively describe a leadership competency or an organizational cultural value. Effective communication in a vibrant high-performance organizational culture is recognized by real dialogue, lots of input, and transparency. *Dialogue implies deeper conversations rather than information handoffs. Dialogue involves demonstrating a true concern for the perspective of others and committing to listening rather than trying to convince* (Yankelovitch 1999). Appreciative exploration gives dialogue its power; people see you care and are willing to invest in hearing them out. Twenty-first century leaders not only enhance their own ability to engender dialogue, but they also enlarge the circle within which organization-wide dialogue can occur. We're not talking about the annual opinion survey or employee suggestion program here. High-performance leadership cultures remove barriers to upward and lateral input and rely less on annual surveys and suggestion programs because leaders ensure the communication exchange is robust throughout the organization.

- When was the last time that you had real dialogue with your organization about its strategic mission, vision, values, and direction?

- Do you have the tendency to answer an associate's question about how to perform a task rather than ask his or her opinion on how he or she could best accomplish it?

- How does the philosophy, "People don't care what you know until they know that you care" apply to your organization? Would your associates agree with the statement applying to you?

- Describe a recent situation in which you engaged in deep dialogue with someone at work. What was that person's reaction?

2. My Opinion Counts: No one likes to feel powerless and unimportant. Giving voice to the diverse wealth of ideas in an organization not only enhances your problem solving and creativity, but also instills an ownership in the workforce missing in many organizational cultures. Everyone has good ideas. A climate of leadership demands input from across the workforce, external customer/constituents, and other organizational partners. We have known for over forty years of research and have been reminded in spades by the recent work by the Gallup organization (Buckingham and Coffman 1999) that *associate commitment to an organization grows as perceptions increase that their opinion counts*. This doesn't have to mean a chaotic mess of disagreement, debate, and argument. It does mean that high-performance leadership cultures find means to garner greater volume and frequency of input from associates as a measure of how things are going and how we can improve. *Feedback is a gift. Ideas are the currency of our next success. Let people see you value both feedback and ideas.*

- How do you react when you receive feedback? Do you get any (not receiving feedback might be indicative of your possible negative reaction to it)?
- Can you recall a recent idea from an associate that led to an important organizational change in direction?
- How does your organization ensure that associates' opinions count?

3. Collaboration: Internal silos challenge nearly every organization. Functional or divisional boundaries can isolate work teams, inhibit effective communication, and reduce creativity. *High-performance cultures demand cross-functional decision making, planning, and support.* They realize that the ability and commitment to share ideas across boundaries is a competitive advantage. They also set high expectations for external collaboration and partnerships so that external talent and intellectual capital can boost the enterprise. Leaders model this behavior and hold managers at all levels accountable for collaboration. *In a high performance culture, "teamness" is pervasive.*

- Are the leaders who surround you committed to interdependency?
- Is this easily recognizable by a "We all own one another's business" attitude of collaboration?
- Have you set performance goals for each individual line of business that clearly reference the overall organizational goals?

4. Integrity: *A corporate culture that doesn't value integrity is forced to endure too much secrecy, risky behavior, conflicts stemming from differing standards for different people, and poor external confidence in the organization.* Much like a parent and child, when top leaders behave in certain ways, the rest of the organization takes that as permission to behave likewise. When top leaders overlook inappropriate behavior in the organization, people soon learn the difference between the written values and the actual code of acceptability. Beyond reproach is the culture you wish.

- How do you communicate your expectation of integrity?
- Do you model it yourself? Impeccably?
- How do you hold other people accountable for integrity?

5. Transparency: A defining characteristic of a culture of leadership is openness and transparency of information and decision-making. As psychologist Virginia

Satir reminds us, "The certainty of misery is more desirable than the misery of uncertainty." *People want to know what's going on, the reasons behind decisions, and what the outlook is: good, bad, or ugly.* People distrust secrecy in organizations. When information is lacking, they become hesitant and frequently hallucinate the worst. More than three decades ago, Peter Drucker coined the acronym "MBWA" (management by walking around), and today most people still know what it stands for. So, most managers know that they need to "walk around" and do so; however, some perform this task without purpose and it's obvious to employees. We see great leaders "walking around" and conducting meaningful dialogue with associates, peers, and customers; seeking advice, input, opinions, and feedback; connecting the dots between work and the organization's mission; and showing real interest in the health and well being of the workforce.

Leadership implies helping people see what you see, facilitating choice based upon what we all see, and also encouraging transparency from the bottom up. Having continuous dialogue with people regarding emerging workplace trends, political relationships, career development, developmental opportunities, and yes, job openings that might take them out of the organization builds tremendous trust and loyalty. Remember the conversations that you had with the best manager you ever worked for/with? It's likely that because of these conversations, you gave him or her your very best, you gave extra effort, and you were loyal. Perhaps you even granted him or her the benefit of the doubt when he or she had to take action prior to discussing it with you. The default position for twenty-first century leaders is creating an environment filled with highly transparent communication.

- How would you describe the communication environment in your organization? How would your associates describe it?
- Can you recall the last real "connection" that you had with an associate while "walking around"?
- Is your default position on transparency set on more rather than less?

6. Accountability: By now, most everyone has heard of General Electric's annual process of identifying the bottom ten percent of performers in all categories and moving them out of the organization. Well, that is one means of signaling accountability. But leaders can also hold people accountable by ensuring clear expectations exist, providing abundant feedback and coaching, and expecting people to deliver on their work promises to their team, their boss, and their customers. Having the right people in the right positions is also critical to accountability. The biggest pressure point for ensuring accountability is in the selection of management leadership. If good ole guys and gals with a knack for political processes seem to be climbing the ladder rather than talented, caring performers, then you're making a statement that accountability doesn't matter that much.

- What messages do you send to your organization regarding accountability?
- Do you rely on only a few "key people" to provide leadership or do you set a consistent standard for everyone to contribute and benefit?
- How are you ensuring your leadership selection process is wide open and competitive for all positions?

7. **Innovation**: Many organizations are still managed by a "Do as I tell you" culture of compliance. Very few, if any, organizations make it to the top and stay there with compliant associates. High-performance organizations have a culture of innovation and creativity where everyone is given permission to think about and question how work is done. Such a culture doesn't happen by spontaneous combustion. Leadership sets the tone for an organization: Will it allow assumptions to be challenged? Is there a spirit of inquiry and critical thinking that's respected and rewarded rather than crushed by management? Are associates taught how to influence upward?

In *The Corporate Fool* (2001), Firth and Allen suggest all organizations need a climate where people "feel free to do the undoable, think the unthinkable, and say the unsayable." Instead of rejecting this creative initiative, leaders open doors to encourage it and teach people how to disagree with diplomacy and influence by making a business case. *Does your workforce perceive they have permission to challenge assumptions, imagine and advance new ideas and suggestions, and process course corrections?* Leaders model a spirit of novelty so that people know that the organization permits and encourages weird ideas and new possibilities. If everyone in your organization keeps talking about needing "out of the box" thinking, then your box may be too small and confining. Contemporary organizations benefit from asymmetrical thinking about how they do business. Leonard and Swap (1999) characterize such a culture of innovation as encouraging "creative abrasion," questioning from a "beginner's mind," and allowing messy creative thinking more like "a plate of spaghetti" than a logical linear process.

- Describe how your organization generates associate commitment vs. compliance.
- Describe the last innovative idea from an associate that made a real difference in the organization. How many can you identify in the past year?

- Do you characterize your organization as having a culture of innovation? How so?

8. Sense of Urgency: Max DePree of Herman Miller once suggested that the "first responsibility of a leader is to define reality" (1990). While we're busy delivering on today's organizational promise, it's easy to overlook how expectations and practices are migrating, or worse yet, deny the changing scene altogether. The landscape in which we work doesn't stand still. Technology is the most vivid example but we also live in a constant state of movement in customer and citizen expectations, global relationships, illegal schemes, as well as what our employees value. If the external environment is always moving, guess what? So too should your organization. Waiting too long and reacting with short spurts of heroic leadership is less healthy than leading and expecting change compatibility everyday. *A sense of urgency about "ongoing transformation" is woven into a culture by leadership that talks about the future with regularity and distributes leadership for change down through the organization.* Leaders ensure that the organization keeps an appropriate sentinel on these shifts and that conversations about shifting external conditions and expectations regularly take place all the way down to work groups. Leaders turn entire organizations into change agents, not just a few key players. By talking about the reality of shifting conditions, the culture maintains an urgency about adapting that's a lot healthier than the panic of surviving.

- What does your organization have a sense of urgency about? Does everyone recognize it?

- How do you continually assess movement in the external environment? How widespread does this occur in the organization?

- What types of conversations are occurring in the organization regarding the future and at what leadership levels are they occurring?

9. Customer/Constituent Focus: We all serve some customer, end user, or constituent whether by service or with product or protection. Older leadership models characterized this relationship as "us" against "them" and the resulting bunker mentality limited thinking and accomplishment. *High-performance cultures ensure there are permeable boundaries between organization and constituent: that is, they engage in lots of conversation, invite ample feedback, and are seen as user-friendly partners.* Twenty-first century leaders see "community" as partners and learn to leverage the vast intellectual and political resources for organizational accomplishment. This requires consistent messages from top leadership, clear expectations for leaders at all levels, and ongoing learning about how to make these challenging external relationships work.

- What is the relationship your organization has with its customers/constituents? How do you continually assess it?
- Do you send a clear message across the organization regarding customer/constituent relationships? What is it?
- How do you seek input and feedback from your customers/constituents? Would they describe it as adequate?
- What changes have you made in the last year based upon customer/constituent input?

10. Learning and Development: So change is constant and we wish to lead a culture of change compatibility. That's where making a stand for ample investment in developing your workforce is critical. *Learning organizations don't see training and learning as an expense. They recognize it as an investment that returns dividends with a workforce that knows you care about their growth and is more greatly attuned to the organization's constant challenge to stay relevant and vibrant.* Yes, you will grow some folks who will take those capabilities elsewhere. However, in the meantime, you've become recognized for your commitment to people, are getting more discretionary effort from the workforce, and are positioned to attract the brightest and best. Remember, the brightest and best always want to be learning. Most organizations adopt the familiar "Our people are our most important resource" slogan. Another version is "Mission first, people always." We're not implying these are wrong, we merely suggest, "Our work is our most important resource to develop our people" as a uniquely different approach.

Leaders with a genuine commitment to associate development are easy to spot. Remember when we earlier related how associates typically respond, "I know it when I see it" when asked about great leadership? Great twenty-first century leaders derive considerable satisfaction from seeing someone else grow and learn. In fact, they typically consider an associate's success more important than their own success and the associate "knows it when he or she sees it." Leaders are always teaching. They take a few moments at the end of every conversation to affirm, tutor, clarify, appreciate, and redirect associates' efforts. This philosophy is ingrained in them and they literally cannot help from doing it because of their own commitment to learning themselves. Great leaders know that when they stop learning they stop leading and they also know the corollary that when they stop teaching they also stop leading.

- What is your organization's commitment to learning and development? Is it evident to the associates at all leadership levels?
- When budgets become tight, does your organization first turn to curb learning and development efforts to reduce costs?
- How would your associates assess your own commitment to learning and development?

Applied Reflection

Leaders Are Learners: Take a moment and jot down some impressions from reading the prior section that may be relevant to your own leadership perspective and growth.

I might need to think differently about how I ...

I might use the following thoughts to better coach other leaders ...

Of all the elements mentioned regarding high-performance leadership cultures, I seem to be strongest at ...

Of all the elements mentioned in this section, it might help to get some advice from others about how I might improve ...

▼

CHAPTER IV

LEADERSHIP LEGACY LESSONS FROM THE RESEARCH

The best organizations and managers gather their strengths together and make their weaknesses irrelevant.

Peter Drucker

Leveraging Success

Many leaders rise through the ranks because supervisors recognize their keen drive and ability to solve problems, to multitask on several simultaneous issues, and to fathom innovative ways to integrate everything to achieve strategic success. They use total quality management, business process reengineering, six sigma principles, and other common management techniques to gain efficiency and improve outcomes. Organizations have come to accept this as a leadership success standard and consequently, many managers have become adept at tirelessly working to identify problems, analyze them, and evaluate optional solutions. Yet, their superiors and stakeholders demand even more, so the next year, they reapply these same principles to eke out incrementally higher results. This focus frequently becomes an exhausting cycle. Many managers even refer to this cycle as leadership success.

Compound these ongoing cycles of initiative and some fad chasing with the fact that we operate in an information-rich world with instant access to one another as well as myriad data of all kind. We recently heard a high-ranking senior executive say that he really appreciates when someone has a clear vision and initiates action to realize it, whether right or wrong. He commented that too often, the senior executive team spends so much time and energy analyzing problems, computing difficult and questionable cost/benefit calculations, and then debating possible solution options that they have very little energy left to actually implement the proposed solution. Perhaps we need a new perspective in the twenty-first century and we need to think and act differently as a result.

A specific characteristic of success recognizable in great leaders in the twenty-first century is their ability to emphasize a few critical and targeted activities that generate "breakthrough" performance improvement rather than attempting a general management approach to a long list of goals. Great leaders study and leverage success to focus on those actions offering the most impact to deliver breakthrough results on the outcomes that really matter. This "leveraging success" approach might actually provide us a different avenue than merely working to correct the organization's perceived weaknesses. Figure 3 (Trinka 2005) indicates the impact on results of applying similar levels of effort toward either "resolving problems" (i.e., correcting weaknesses) or "leveraging success" (i.e., building upon strengths). Emphasizing problem solving most frequently brings only incremental improvement, while leveraging strengths and successes may offer the type of "breakthrough" results sought by most enterprises. We don't imply that a problem-solving focus is wrong. We only believe that many leaders don't "think differently" and consider the possible implications and breakthrough results that emerge from a strategy focused on "leveraging success." So we suggest a "both/and" philosophy since we know that a "leveraging success" approach is so rarely attempted.

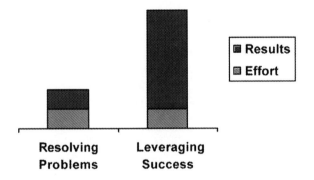

Figure 3: Incremental vs. Breakthrough Results

What's a Manager to Do?

Many organizations conduct periodic surveys that probe employee, and sometimes customer, attitudes and opinions relating to productivity, profitability, retention, and satisfaction. In their groundbreaking book, *First Break All the Rules*, Marcus Buckingham and Curt Coffman (1999), in collaboration with the Gallup Organization, devised a set of twelve questions that most accurately measure the strength of a workplace (employee engagement). After studying the most successful companies and the factors that reveal loyal, productive, and engaged employees, Buckingham and Coffman argue that the number one reason why people thrive in an organization is their immediate supervisor. It's also the number one reason employees quit. Their research has clearly established the high correlation between strong employee engagement and increased productivity and results—most often based on the leader's effectiveness. So, unless we're missing something, we believe that important outcomes for any organization are delivered through strong employee engagement and effective leadership.

We seek to simplify the life of a busy manager and provide insight into determining which specific leadership competencies and activities are most important and answer the tantalizing question, "What's a manager to do?" By studying and leveraging success and recognizing and appreciating what works for great leaders and organizations, we can determine the "vital few" competencies and activities that have the most impact on generating "breakthrough" results and possibly accelerating legacies to take root.

Differentiating Leadership Competencies

It's not particularly insightful to assert that great leaders make a great difference in any type of organization. We all know that great leaders balance their roles and responsibilities across many core management areas and even more leadership competencies. In our leadership presentations, we usually ask our audiences to imagine the best leader that they ever worked for or with. We then ask participants to cite the strengths that differentiated that leader from others. Interestingly, the strengths that these participants cite typically relate to only a few very important characteristics of business skills (e.g., decisiveness, intelligence, drive) and interpersonal skills (e.g., developing others, empathy, communication). Then participants report that, yes, these leaders have weaknesses as well, but "their strengths overshadow their weaknesses." Most people state that the best leaders they have worked for or with are known more for a few powerful strengths than an absence of weaknesses. So, we conclude that most great leaders are not superheroes. Most great leaders normally possess only a few profound strengths that they leverage to achieve outstanding results, despite some weaknesses. We also think differently and suggest that a "building strengths" approach of growing leaders may offer more return than the typical "correcting weaknesses" approach followed by most organizations. Knowing this, we might ask: What characteristics or competencies differentiate great leaders from the rest? On which core strengths should we focus? On which core strengths should we encourage our managers to concentrate for development? Few have answered these simple questions.

Another question that many organizations and leaders ask revolves around the efficacy of leadership development in general. The classic "Are leaders born or made?" argument surfaces at this point, which some organizations use to rationalize a lack of emphasis in this area. If indeed some of you believe leaders are born, then you would also most likely conclude that few organizations have enough born leaders. Informal research that we've done suggests that people believe the number of born leaders may only range from eight to ten percent of the entire leadership population. Therefore, most of our organizations need to develop more leaders to ensure sufficient numbers to fill key positions. For organizations and leaders interested in developing others, our challenge is how to establish an effective environment to grow more successful leaders.

Analyzing successful leaders and building leaders' strengths have recently generated a lot of enthusiasm. In *The Extraordinary Leader,* Jack Zenger and Joe Folkman (2002) provide compelling evidence that turning our good leaders (the 60–80 percent in the vast middle) into great ones has a much greater impact on business results than just correcting the weaknesses of our worst leaders. We also now have a better understanding of what differentiates great leaders (defined as those in the top 10 percent) from others, offering us exciting new avenues for developing more great leaders.

A Look at the Data on Strength Building

Many good managers lament that they don't have the time to become great and that, after all, good is good enough isn't it? In fact, we often see a manager's 360-degree assessment results displayed against "average" scores for each competency, which unknowingly perpetuates leadership mediocrity. In many ways, good has become the enemy of excellent and we must challenge ourselves to develop our leaders into something more than just average (Collins 2001). Studying the 360-degree assessments of over two thousand public sector managers reveals some very interesting results on the competencies that differentiate great leaders in the top 10 percent from the rest.

For example, even though the organizations in the study have a comprehensive list of numerous desired leadership competencies, only about half of those characteristics differentiate the best leaders from the rest. Interestingly, these key differentiating competencies typically balance across core management areas such as leadership, employee engagement, customer focus, achieving results, and building relationships (see Table 4). You might notice that a few common competencies are missing, for example—integrity/honesty. We certainly don't imply that concepts like integrity/honesty and teamwork (also absent) are not important, since they are crucial competencies for leaders to possess. It's just that because the vast majority of managers score very highly in these competencies on 360-degree assessments, these areas do not "differentiate" great leaders from the rest. And since it is often better to be distinct rather than extinct, the implication is that you are better off focusing on the differentiators.

Core Management Areas				
Leadership	Employee Engagement	Customer Focus	Achieving Results	Building Relationships
Communication	Develops Others	Genuinely Listens	Achieves Goals	Collaboration
Critical, Strategic Thinking	Constructive Feedback	Partnering	Political Savvy	Leverages Diversity
Champions Change				

Table 4: Key "Differentiating" Competencies

Furthermore, managers who display profound strength (scores in the top 10 percent of their peers on that particular item) in only four of these key differentiating competencies achieve overall leadership effectiveness levels in the top 10 percent. This confirms our common sense experience that one does not need to be a superhero to be identified as a great leader. The empirical evidence of this study also confirms the value of diversity in leaders, as strengths in *any four* of the key differentiating competencies engendered perceptions of great leadership. In fact, most people cite only three to four profound strengths when they think of the best leader that they have ever worked for or with. Most also quickly point out that that same leader's weaknesses don't matter because his or her strengths are so profound. In effect, the presence of a few profound strengths creates a "halo effect" that overshadows any perceived weaknesses.

The concept of key differentiating competencies implies that leaders can now focus developmental resources on improving a shorter list of competencies instead of diffusing training efforts on an organization's entire list of leadership competencies. Most managers remark that they don't have time to focus on development anyway and besides, they are aware that previous efforts have not proved particularly effective. Instead of lengthening an already time-pressed manager's "to do" list, this study offers a method of focusing that list to include only those items that are likely to have the greatest impact on improving leadership effectiveness and business results. The twenty-first century leadership and legacy concepts discussed in this book are influenced by this research as we seek to focus your attention on those areas that have the most impact on improving both employee productivity and overall leadership effectiveness. By thinking differently about leadership impact, you might consider breaking out of the management cycle of applying the same old type of business process reengineering year in and year out. Leadership is different from management and we might derive even greater return on a focused leadership development approach.

The Error in Identifying Weaknesses as Developmental Targets

Traditional development methods focus on correcting weaknesses and at best, produce only incremental improvement. This research shows that correcting a manager's weaknesses only increases performance about 10 percent with only marginal increases in business results. After all, we're asking managers to improve on activities that they aren't particularly good at, don't enjoy performing (perhaps dislike doing), and that others confirm they don't do very well. This doesn't sound like a particularly successful prescription for improvement, yet that's exactly the guidance that most organizations provide managers. Many try to mask this practice by using language such as focusing on "challenges" or "developmental opportunities," but it's transparent that we are attempting to correct a leader's weaknesses and that approach, subtle or not, conveys distinctly negative connotations.

As a result of the Zenger and Folkman study, and in a much more positive light, we encourage leaders to build at least one more of the key differentiating competencies that others already identify as a strong area (80th percentile) to an even higher level above the 90th percentile. This innovative method attempts to take advantage of the power of perception and create a "halo effect" for that manager where others value his or her strengths so much that they overshadow any weaknesses. Rather than feeling pressure and guilt about correcting weaknesses, a leader experiences the positive energy generated by an identification and further development of his or her strengths, which generates considerable motivation for behavioral change. Is this simply perception management or real leadership impact, you might ask? The research shows that adding just one more strength delivers as much as an 80 percent improvement in overall leadership effectiveness and business results (Zenger and Folkman 2002).

Profound Weaknesses

At this point, a few of you may be skeptical, since you remember working for some very bad managers and realize that this approach probably would not have worked in those cases. The research shows that you're right to a degree and we have to approach these cases in a slightly different manner. When thinking about the worst leader that people have worked for or with, most cite the presence of only one or two profound weaknesses or fatal flaws that overshadow any strengths that the individual may possess. Profound weaknesses stand out either as low, outlying scores on 360-degree reports or as mediocre scores in areas critically important to a leader's specific job (e.g., influencing/negotiating for a labor relations manager). Certainly, to improve others' perceptions of that person's leadership, he or she must correct those fatal flaws. However, our research indicates that the vast majority of leaders (75 percent) do not exhibit fatal flaws and that an emphasis on building strengths is as much as eight times more effective (80 percent vs. 10 percent) than correcting weaknesses (Trinka 2004, 2005)!

The Role of Companion Competencies

This study reveals another very important concept that offers a unique approach for improving behavior associated with targeted competencies, even those that may indicate a fatal flaw. Previous methods of improving a certain competency usually focus on a direct developmental approach. In other words, if a person targeted technical credibility as a competency to improve, we would probably send him or her to technical school for further development. As it turns out, other people's perceptions of and confidence in one's technical credibility are influenced not simply by technical knowledge, but also by a few other closely related (companion) competencies. This research indicates that other people's perceptions of interpersonal skills (e.g., develops others) and business skills (e.g., strategic thinking) are very closely correlated with perceptions of technical credibility. So, technically competent managers have the best chance of being seen by others as technically credible when they use good interpersonal skills to display their technical credibility and apply their technical skills in a strategic way (i.e., do not micromanage their employees).

This companion competency concept potentially revolutionizes leadership development efforts for both individual and group customization. Even in the case of a fatal flaw, developing around the targeted competency by focusing on closely related companion competencies often proves more effective at raising leadership strength in that area than a direct developmental approach. And in most cases, focusing development on companion competencies actually raises the perceptions of a leader's behavior associated with many other competencies as well, which raises his or her overall leadership effectiveness to levels similar to those of the organization's best leaders. So, for individual managers, we recommend building strengths using companion competencies and leveraging the "halo effect" where a few profound strengths counterbalance an individual leader's lesser competencies to achieve breakthrough performance improvement leadership.

Key Companion Competencies

For group customization of leadership development efforts, the research in our study uncovers a list of only five companion competencies (Develops Others; Critical, Strategic Thinking; Champions Change; Achieves Goals; and Collaboration) that deliver development on all of the key competencies that differentiate great leaders from the rest. This finding implies that we can refocus a dauntingly long list of competencies to a much shorter list of key characteristics that our great leaders possess and then develop just five of those to have the greatest development impact on all of the differentiators. We have now made the problem much more manageable from an individual leader's perspective and can make good leaders great without lengthening their "to do" list.

Good does not equal "great," and all organizations need more great leaders. Our research evidence suggests great leaders are not superheroes and that developing more great leaders involves leveraging the power of perception by building a leader's key differentiating strengths to even higher levels to counterbalance weaknesses. We also learned that, when building strengths or even for correcting significant flaws, most times it's more effective to develop closely related companion competencies rather than using the traditional direct development approach.

The best use of these innovative leadership development techniques is customizing an action plan to improve the overall leadership effectiveness of an individual leader who has just received feedback through a 360-degree assessment. A secondary use is to design group offerings for managers using the few companion competencies that offer development on all of the key differentiators. Either way, we offer evidence on a plan to more efficiently and effectively develop leadership that provides a very powerful business case for both the participant manager and the organizational units investing precious capital in leadership development.

Leadership and Employee Productivity

Over the past few years, we've had access to numerous surveys dealing with employee performance and productivity, employee development, and leadership effectiveness. The ones that we find particularly interesting often study successful leaders and hone in on the characteristics and competencies that differentiate great leaders from the rest and focus on what is working. As mentioned, we find this approach much more positive than the opposite approach that probes weaknesses and what isn't working. It's also clear to us that we don't identify our best leaders by an absence of shortcomings, but rather by the attributes and competencies that lead to their success and what does work. Moreover, focusing on success creates positive energy by recognizing and appreciating what is working, which seems to produce greater engagement and momentum for change.

When we reviewed numerous surveys (Corporate Executive Board 2002, 2003, 2004, 2005, 2006) on topics important to employee engagement and productivity, we noticed unusual similarities in findings and recommendations. We viewed these similarities as undeniable and we realized that the associates who completed these surveys conscientiously filled them out in the "hope" for positive workplace changes in leadership and culture. We regularly hear associates complain that few things actually change as a result of these survey efforts, so we strive to amplify their voices that eagerly yearn for better leadership.

The "vital few" competencies of develops others, results-driven performance, and communication resurfaced repeatedly to differentiate leaders who achieved the highest levels of employee productivity (Trinka 2005). Specifically, the evidence supports the establishment of a high-performance leadership culture (results-driven performance), not from a command and control perspective, but one that involves the establishment of a learning environment (develops others) with a conscious focus on continuous dialogue within work teams (communication): twenty-first century leadership. Furthermore, managers who undertake specific activities related to this approach have a much better chance of achieving "breakthrough" employee performance improvements, leading to "breakthrough" results for the organization. Let's look at this approach more closely.

Develops Others

Few managers would disagree on the importance of their crucial role in coaching and mentoring employees and many spend a considerable amount of their valuable time on employee development activities. In early 2003, the Corporate Leadership Council's Learning and Development Roundtable analyzed survey responses from nearly 8,500 employees and their managers on a wide range of employee development activities. The results confirm that a vast majority of managers (three out of four) agree that coaching and mentoring their employees is crucial to organizational success and report spending about 15–20 percent of their time on employee development activities. However, the results also indicate that employees rate their managers barely above average (4.05 out of 7.0) on their effectiveness in this role. Furthermore, most managers do not see a significant return on their time investment (Corporate Executive Board 2003).

By examining the employee development activities of the highest rated managers, we see that some activities have a much more positive influence on improving employee engagement than others. Statistical estimates show that improving a manager's effectiveness at employee development can positively influence employee retention and satisfaction by as much as 40 percent, commitment by as much as 30 percent, and productivity by as much as 20 percent (Corporate Executive Board 2003). The evidence is even more staggering for senior leaders who are the best at developing their subordinate managers. These managers are 25 percent more likely to stay, 33 percent more engaged, give 35 percent more discretionary effort, and experience 27 percent higher employee performance and productivity (Corporate Executive Board 2006). These are breakthrough results!

Survey responses show some fascinating disparities in perceptions between employees and managers concerning employee development. The vast majority of employees seek to learn and grow in the course of doing day-to-day work and want their managers to create a learning environment in that context. On the other hand, many managers report a lack of confidence to perform well in that role. Armed with the results of this research and organizational support, managers can proceed with much more confidence in performing specifically targeted employee development activities and the business case is compelling.

We encourage leaders to establish an environment and strategy to support continuous on-the-job learning. The good news for busy managers is that associates want to learn more on-the-job and blur the line between learning and work. Too often, we hear of organizations and managers who exclusively focus on external development programs or worse yet, outsource the job of employee development to the organization's internal training division. Leaders need to create an environment where learning flourishes at work. We suggest actions such as handing out work assignments with a clear explanation of why that associate was selected for the task and how they can use or hone their unique talents on it, answering associate questions with a "What do you think?" response instead of a quick answer, and displaying how the organization can best act to meet individual aspirations through collaboration. We again ask you to think of the best leader you worked for or with and recall the dialogue you had with that person regarding your development. Our experience suggests that most people describe how that leader had considerable confidence and trust in their abilities and set challenging goals for them to develop and realize their full potential.

Results-driven Performance

All managers agree on the importance of employee productivity and business results and would probably rate themselves fairly proficient in providing performance feedback. In mid-2002, the Corporate Executive Board's Learning and Development Roundtable analyzed survey responses from nearly twenty thousand employees and managers on a wide range of manager-related activities involving employee performance (Corporate Executive Board 2003). Overall, managers received a poor report card on these activities as only 30–40 percent of employees agreed that their managers communicated performance standards and provided fair and accurate feedback to help them do their jobs better.

Interestingly, most of the performance improvement activities that managers can utilize (e.g., providing specific suggestions for doing the job better, detailing the amount of effort to put into a job, and diffusing unhealthy rivalries and competition, etc.) have minimal impact on individual employee productivity. The results clearly show that managers have a much better chance of vastly improving employee productivity by targeting their efforts on a much smaller list of activities. In fact, managers who set clear performance standards, become more knowledgeable about employee performance, and provide fair and accurate informal feedback on performance strengths can significantly improve individual productivity. After all, the first question on the Gallup Q12 employee engagement survey is, "I know what is expected of me at work" (Buckingham and Coffman 1999). And when discussing weaknesses, managers who clearly focus on specific suggestions for improvement or development can improve employee performance. Conversely, those who exclusively emphasize weaknesses most often dramatically decrease performance. In short, managers who provide feedback that is voluntary, detailed, immediate, and positive can positively influence employee productivity (Corporate Executive Board 2003).

This information shouldn't surprise most of us as we've heard it all before and it seems intuitive. However, survey responses again show some disparities in perceptions between employees and managers. The majority of employees believe that formal performance reviews do nothing to actually help their on-the-job performance, yet they crave voluntary and detailed informal performance feedback, especially on strengths. Interestingly, the majority of managers view formal performance reviews as an administrative requirement rather than as an influential lever to positively influence employee productivity. In fact, many managers report that they specifically cite performance weaknesses to lower an employee's rating below the highest mark rather than emphasizing strengths to raise performance ratings above minimally successful. On informal feedback, employees report that most managers provide general praise, rather than specific and detailed recognition.

We don't mean to imply that managers can never mention or speak to employees about weaknesses, in effect being "easy" on them. Again, recall the conversations that you had with the best leader you worked for or with. Was that manager easy on you? We mostly hear that great leaders are neither "easy" nor "soft" on their employees. In fact, they're tough because they set high standards, yet also show high confidence in their associates' ability to achieve more than they think they can. Most often, we hear from associates that their best leaders considered the associate's success more important than their own success and the associate "knew it when he or she saw it."

Communication

In 1968, Peter Drucker coined the acronym, MBWA, or management by walking around. This concept has become so universal that new managers almost instinctively know that they need to "walk around" to achieve high effectiveness levels. Unfortunately, they may not have specific objectives or topic areas in mind for the conversations they have with their associates while they walk around. In general, that might be all right, but we offer some additional suggestions. In his recent book, *The One Thing You Need to Know*, Marcus Buckingham (2005) advises managers to seek to turn talent into performance and discover what's unique in each individual and capitalize on it. He also encourages leaders to rally people to a better future by providing clarity on what the organization considers universally important and crucial to its existence. We strongly believe such clarity reduces uncertainty concerning the future, reduced uncertainty leads to higher engagement, higher engagement means more effective leadership, and better leadership delivers improved outcomes.

We suggest that leaders need to say, "This is where we're going" (paint a vivid picture of a successful future for the organization and its employees) and specifically cite why he or she needs each person to get there. When either of us reflect back on our business careers, we don't recall many instances where we heard this type of message and if we had, we also know what kind of impact it might have had. Imagine a leader vividly and confidently describing the future and then specifically explaining to you why he or she needed you to get there. That would have kept either of us engaged for months! Again, we recall the conversations we had with the best leaders that we worked for or with. We realized that person was preoccupied with making us successful and because of that, we did our very best, we committed more of our discretionary effort, we were loyal, and we trusted that he or she had our best interests in mind when making quick decisions without our input. Because of their emphasis on us, we reciprocated with intense productivity and enjoyed it, even though it might have been exhausting.

The "Vital Few" Competencies

The research studies that we are citing begin to coalesce. Common conclusions create a compelling business case for concentrating effort on managerial and leadership competencies with the most impact relating to developing others, results-driven performance, and communication. However, most people believe that the leadership perspective of their profession is unique and that a shorter list of "vital few" leadership competencies does not completely apply to their environment. Upon further review of our research studying various employee surveys and managerial 360-degree assessments, we've discovered that the similarities among various professions' leadership perspectives far outweigh whatever minimal differences might exist. For others, this approach either seems too simple or appears to offer little new insight. We quickly point out that although our "vital few" competencies might appear simplistic or rudimentary, our experience tells us that employees don't rate managers very high in these areas. A 2005 Merit Systems Protection Board (MSPB) survey found that less than half of over thirty-seven thousand federal employees view their supervisors as a resource for improving workplace skills (Rutzick 2006). Another recent government-wide survey revealed that only 35 percent of employees view their organization's leaders effective at generating workforce motivation and commitment (Partnership for Public Service and the Institute for the Study of Public Policy Implementation 2004).

As a result, we have formulated a visual depiction of our research conclusions (Figure 5) that shows the relationships among what we view as *foundational competencies*, the *"vital few" accelerators*, and the *outcomes* that we're most interested in. In general, our leadership perspective is characterized by the possession of a few *foundational competencies* of personal character, such as integrity/honesty, self assurance, professionalism, and service motivation, which serve as critical selection criteria and probably cannot be improved much by leadership training.

Few would argue the belief that a strong and solid base of personal character must underlie leaders in every profession. Some highly publicized cases of a leader's lack of integrity have recently undermined the credibility of leadership in general and left a lasting impression of the great importance of personal character. In their study of over twenty-five thousand public and private sector managers, Jack Zenger and Joe Folkman (2002) find that displaying personal character through high integrity and honesty forms the basis of strong leadership and acts like the center pole of a tent that must be raised prior to and higher than the outer poles or leadership characteristics.

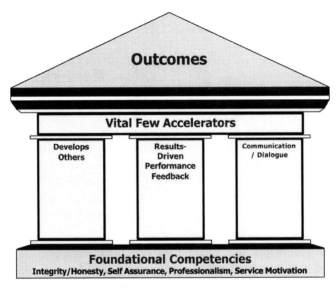

Figure 5: Legacy Leadership Model

Our great leaders use this foundation as a solid base and apply a *"vital few"* *accelerating competencies* to achieve the *outcomes* crucial to their organization's success. For example, by focusing on improving the behaviors associated with "Develops Others," "Results-driven Performance Feedback," and "Communication/Dialogue" competencies, managers can increase overall leadership effectiveness scores by 50–60 percent (Trinka 2005). The associated behaviors of these competencies are: 1) creates an environment and strategy to support continuous on-the-job learning, 2) clarifies performance expectations and gives timely, constructive feedback on tasks and assignments, and 3) strategically uses communication to produce enthusiasm and foster an atmosphere of open exchange, support, and trust. For us, the desired *outcomes* of employee engagement and leadership effectiveness are worthy of considerable value. We offer this model of leadership legacy for others to emulate for success.

As further evidence of the efficacy or our model, we studied the results of a Gallup Q12 employee engagement survey with over eighty thousand respondents in a large government agency and discovered that five of the twelve questions differentiated the best workgroups (top 10 percent) from the rest (Trinka 2005). Similar to the results of previously cited research and surveys, managers have a much better chance of vastly improving the workplace environment for their employees by targeting efforts on a much smaller list of performance drivers. By listing the five key differentiating questions, we clearly see patterns of what survey respondents are telling their managers to focus on.

√ In the last seven days, I have received recognition or praise for doing good work.

√ At work, my opinions seem to count.

√ There is someone at work who encourages my development.

√ This last year, I have had opportunities at work to learn and grow.

√ In the last six months, someone at work has talked to me about my progress.

Two of these questions relate to conversations about performance, two others speak directly to the value of employee development activities, and the last implies an atmosphere of open exchange and support thus again validating the "vital few" competencies approach. By separating the survey responses by managers and employees, we see some disparities in perceptions concerning employee engagement. A vast majority of employees want someone at work (usually their managers) to conduct dialogues on performance, mission importance and alignment with organizational goals, emerging work trends, and career development. On the other hand, many managers do not believe that their employees want them to discuss these issues. The implications of this disparity clearly stand out when we compare the business results of the highest scoring workgroups to those with the lowest scores (remember, managerial effectiveness is the number one reason that employees thrive in an organization). In one retail chain, Buckingham and Coffman (1999) found that workgroups who scored in the top 25 percent ended the year almost 5 percent over their sales budget while those scoring in the bottom 25 percent were nearly 1 percent below budget, which amounted to a difference of one hundred and four million dollars. Profit/loss sheets and employee turnover comparisons pointed to an even more dramatic impact of scoring in the top 25 percent.

Common Activities Associated with the "Vital Few"

An overwhelming body of evidence exists to highlight the important and vital role of a manager's leadership competencies on employee productivity and retention. We have shown evidence on the value of focusing on a "vital few" accelerating competencies to engender increased employee productivity and business results. We realize that these competencies represent more general concepts than specific recommendations on potentially useful activities, so we seek to offer some practical advice as well. Questions often arise about which managerial activities have the most impact on improving employee performance and what the extent of that improvement is. However, the potential list of activities that a manager can undertake to improve employee performance and productivity is as long as the oceans are wide. Thus, we evaluate a long list of managerial activities to determine the much smaller number of those activities that have the most impact on improving both employee productivity and leadership effectiveness, ultimately achieving dramatic increases in organizational results. While the approach of focusing on "what's working" to lead organizational change is not new (Hammond 1996) the application of this focus to leadership assessment and development is relatively new (Zenger and Folkman 2002).

After reviewing the impact of over 250 possible managerial activities, we suggest a short list of only ten that has the most potential for delivering high employee productivity improvement, since these differentiate great leaders from the rest. By studying success and recognizing and appreciating what works for great leaders, we can determine the actions that have the most impact on both employee productivity and leadership effectiveness. And the best news is that busy managers may be able to decrease emphasis on some of the activities we have done in the past that have the least impact. In other words, we can create "stop doing" lists to supplement our edited "to do" lists to ensure that remaining activities have maximum impact.

Given the vast range of responsibilities and activities that managers can undertake, we think that any method of simplifying a time-pressed manager's life is worthwhile, especially if we can cite specific evidence in support of a few key concepts. In that light, we have summarized the results of the previously cited surveys around the common themes that emerge involving employee development, employee performance, and communication. Table 6 depicts the most influential activities, grouped by these three common themes, in descending order of their impact on a combined index of employee engagement and leadership effectiveness. Overall, activities involving employee development have the highest average impact on employee productivity and leadership effectiveness at 33.3 percent, employee performance averages 28.5 percent, and communication comes in a close third at 25.7 percent.

Employee Development	Employee Performance	Communication
Leaders act as good role models for developing employees.	Leader is knowledgeable about employee performance.	Leaders genuinely listen to employees and value their opinions (dialogue).
Leaders encourage employee development and make it a priority.	Leaders provide voluntary, detailed, immediate, and positive informal feedback.	Leaders clearly communicate expectations and standards.
Leaders ensure each project or assignment is a learning experience for employees.	Leaders recognize and emphasize employee strengths.	Leaders pass along job and development opportunities.
Leaders help employees apply new skills and knowledge on-the-job.	Leaders regularly appreciate employee contributions and accomplishment	Leaders share information employees need to understand and trust the organization

Table 6: Most Influential Managerial Activities

Great leaders provide a confident and vivid description of successful end goals and determine ways to assess progress and celebrate wins along the way. They assign the right people to the right task to turn talent into performance and figure out how to develop existing skill gaps on-the-job. And finally, they connect the dots for associates by showing how the work supports the organization's mission and vision, how it will develop participants, and how everyone's opinion will count.

High-Performance Leadership Culture

Facing a continuing competitive economic environment and intense scrutiny of leadership bench strength, most organizations currently place great emphasis on succession management and plan to increase investment in leadership development in the future. Organizations increasingly require effective leaders to move forward, regardless of sector (public, private, or non-profit), industry, or cyclical economic/budget fluctuations. In 2003, Accenture (Corporate Executive Board 2003) surveyed over one thousand CEOs and discovered that five of the top seven corporate priorities related to workforce and leadership quality (Figure 7). In addition, the President's Management Agenda (2002) cites the importance of leadership as a crucial driver of strategic government human capital management.

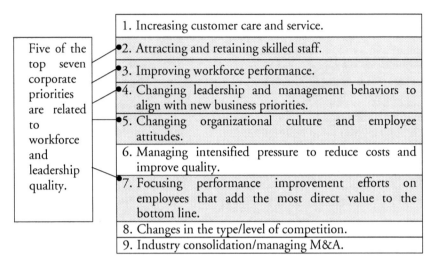

	1. Increasing customer care and service.
Five of the top seven corporate priorities are related to workforce and leadership quality.	●2. Attracting and retaining skilled staff.
	●3. Improving workforce performance.
	●4. Changing leadership and management behaviors to align with new business priorities.
	●5. Changing organizational culture and employee attitudes.
	6. Managing intensified pressure to reduce costs and improve quality.
	●7. Focusing performance improvement efforts on employees that add the most direct value to the bottom line.
	8. Changes in the type/level of competition.
	9. Industry consolidation/managing M&A.

Figure 7: Top Corporate Strategic Priorities

Unfortunately, the near-universal agreement about the criticality of leadership is not matched by universal agreement among organizations on how to develop effective leaders. If leadership development is so important, why is there such a lack of consensus about how to effectively achieve it? Most organizations comment that they have too few leaders to address the challenge of executive succession, insufficient resources for creating an effective leadership development strategy, and an incomplete understanding of what issues to focus on. Ironically, the challenge facing organizations to design and implement an effective leadership development strategy is not a lack of viable ideas but the converse, an overwhelming number of plausible ideas and approaches and little empirical or systematic evidence with which to sort out decisions. We seek to help organizations make sense of this baffling landscape and allocate (or reallocate) scarce leadership development resources to optimally establish and maintain a high-performance leadership culture. Organizations shouldn't have to choose a leadership development strategy based on intuition and anecdotal evidence. They should base decisions for building the desired leadership culture on empirical evidence rather than guesswork, anecdotes, or hunches. Due to limited resources, organizations must make the right choices to develop their leaders, optimally focusing their scarce time, effort, and monetary resources on the point of greatest return.

In 2003, the Corporate Executive Board's Corporate Leadership Council analyzed succession management survey responses from managers in 276 organizations worldwide. The survey revealed insights into the criteria (competencies) that have the greatest impact on improving potential successor identification and development. Table 8 depicts the results, to include the empirical impact (in percent) on improving leadership quality. Key criteria for successor identification and development include integrity/honesty and group leadership (crucial to employee performance), developing others, and communication. A glance at the table also suggests a needed balance between interpersonal and business skills. Improving managers' performance in these activities/competencies will undoubtedly steer the organization's leadership culture to support the CEO's workforce and leadership quality initiatives and subsequently drive "breakthrough" improvements in organizational results.

Successor Identification Criteria		Successor Development Criteria	
Integrity/Honesty	38.5%	Group Leadership	42.2%
Developing Others	37.3%	Entrepreneurship	38.1%
Diversity Awareness	35.2%	Decisiveness	35.9%
Technical Credibility	34.1%	Strategic Thinking	34.5%
Business Acumen	33.8%	Customer Focus	33.9%
Communication	32.9%	Problem Solving	33.1%
Political Savvy	32.8%		
Interpersonal Skills	30.6%		

Table 8: Most Influential Leadership Competencies

So, we've learned that by focusing on just a few recommended competencies and activities, organizations can greatly improve both workforce and leadership quality, which is very high on the list of CEO top priorities and for good reason. In their excellent work, *When Teams Work Best,* Frank LaFasto and Carl Larson (2002) show that companies with "top tier" leadership quality (great leaders) outperform their competitors in revenue margins by over 500 percent, in net income by over 700 percent, and in stock price performance by over 800 percent. As we suspected, a manager's, or maybe we should say a leader's, role does have a significant impact on employee productivity and we offer specific, empirically justified suggestions for improvement. It seems we can use hard science to help apply and build the soft skill of leadership!

Legacy Impact

The paradox at the heart of organizational leadership is that the leader must add value to the organization but must not take it away when he or she leaves. An essential part of a leader's job is to become dispensable through creating a *culture of leadership* that extends throughout the organization. When an organization becomes incapable and falls apart after the leader departs, the subsequent ruin is, in a sense, a validation of that leader's talent and evidence of the value added during his or her tenure. But it is also evidence of that leader's failure to endow the organization with the qualities needed to transcend previous achievements, to nurture the conditions under which leadership can flourish, and to leave a leadership legacy behind. Some leaders fail to create a culture of leadership, and instead foster a personal cult. A cult is a rudimentary, incomplete, inherently ephemeral phenomenon that fades when the personality that creates it departs. A culture is much more durable and robust than a cult, because its survival and power do not depend on the presence and personality of a single individual.

Applied Reflection

Leaders Are Learners: Take a moment and jot down some impressions from reading the prior section that may be relevant to your own leadership perspective and growth.

I might need to think differently about how I ...

I might use the following thoughts to better coach other leaders ...

Of all the elements mentioned from the research perspective, I seem to be most aligned with ...

Of all the elements mentioned in this section, it might help to get some advice from others about how I might improve ...

CHAPTER V

▼

A LEGACY IMPORTANT TO WHERE YOU ARE

Being a leader brings with it a responsibility to do something of significance that makes families, communities, work organizations, nations, the environment, and the world better places than they are today.

James Kouzes and Barry Posner, 2006

Why Legacy?

You are leaving a legacy of leadership whether you like it or not and whether it's good or not. Take this opportunity to reflect, assess, and focus what you really wish your leadership legacy to be.

What is a Legacy?

A legacy is not simply "how you hope you're remembered." Leadership legacy is about the climate of leadership and the capability of the organization and other leaders in it to sustain a culture of twenty-first century leadership after a great leader is gone because of efforts he or she made while he or she was there. What impact on leadership did you create in the time you had? What leadership climate is important to leave behind in the organization?

"You Can't Teach Old Dogs New Tricks"

(Senior Government Executive since Retired November 2004)

We don't know if we're bringing lots of new, new leadership concepts and perspectives to you. However, we do know that leaders are learners and stay committed to

52

learning their entire career. Leaders continue to engage in growing their understanding about who they are and what contemporary leadership looks like. These characteristics of leaders are well written about in the "personal mastery" and "authentic leadership" literature (Covey 1989; Senge 1990; George 2003; Avolio and Luthans 2006). Senge writes, "Personal mastery goes beyond competence and skills ... it means approaching one's life as a creative work, living life from a creative as opposed to a reactive viewpoint."

Personal mastery is enhanced by continually asking, "What is leadership?" "How am I leading?" "What impact am I making?" The following exercises might help you reflect and focus on being the best leader you can be. We have already asked you to assess how you're adapting your leadership to the contemporary challenges of your enterprise. You may believe there are not many new tricks left for you. However, there are always new levels of focus, prioritization, adaptation, and recommitment that leaders constantly make. We believe that's what twenty-first century leaders continually ask of themselves.

What Processes Might be Helpful?

- Take the time to reflect on you and your organization's current challenges and climate of leadership.
- Engage your peers to learn about their perspectives on organizational challenges and their experiences with such challenges.

Consider how to focus and execute your leadership to even greater impact:

- Realize that whether excellent or mediocre as a leader, you are teaching others how to lead and impacting a climate of leadership that will help or hurt the organization when you leave. What do you want your leadership legacy to be?
- Think back over what you consider to be "defining moments" in your understanding of leadership and your capabilities to lead. What were the circumstances, and who were the significant people involved?

The following reflective exercises may help you think through the "legacy" concept by exploring what your core values and competencies might be and considering which ones require your focus if they are to become embedded in the culture such that they remain after you leave: a leadership legacy.

Targeting an Important Legacy Where You Are

Reflection: What Legacy Will You Leave with Your People/ Organization?

What leadership values/characteristics do you wish to leave with your organization?	Why are these "critical" enough to become your leadership legacy focus?
What?	Why?
1.	1.
2.	2.
3.	3.
4.	4.
5.	5.

Reflection: What Legacies Do You Remember?

Think of a leader/person who taught you, or a learning situation or defining moment from which you learned these values/characteristics?	What happened?/How did you learn?
Parents/Grandparents/Siblings/Spouse	
Teachers/Coaches	
Spiritual/Religious Leader	
Boss/Superior Officer/Peer	
Mentor/Leadership Coach	
Trusted Friend	
Direct Reports/Employee Associates	
Management Experience	
Crisis	
Setback/Failure	
Challenging Project/Assignment	
Reading/Formal Study	

Reflection: What Have You Learned About Leadership?

What do the experts say about leadership that describes the values/characteristics you've chosen as a legacy focus? This might alert you to an area for further reading and study. Consult our list of references at the end of this book for potential resources.
1.
2.
3.
4.
5.

Reflection: What Actions Will Ensure Your Leadership Legacy?

What can/will/are you doing to ensure these legacies become embedded in the leadership culture of your organization? Revisit this section after you've read and reflected on Chapter VI.
1.
2.
3.
4.
5.

Chapter VI

▼

Ensuring a Leadership Legacy Strategy

The future is not a result of choices
among alternative paths offered by the present,
but a place that is created,
first in mind,
next in will, then in activity.

The future is not some place we are going to,
But a place we are creating.

The paths are not to be discovered, but made,
And the activity of making the future changes
Both the maker and the destination.

John Schaar

Leaders leave legacies. They impact an organization, work team, or individuals in ways that have lasting marks on culture and values, how people work together, and the growth of individuals. As a leader, your time is finite and shouldn't be squandered. Whether measured in years or shorter cycles, leaders always leave legacies: some huge, some small, some healthy, some less so. But they always leave a legacy.

We ask you to consider the primary channels through which leaders leave their fingerprints on organizations and people. This list is not exhaustive; it's merely suggestive of how leaders can cause positive leadership climates to take roots. What is the context of 90 percent of your day? How much attention do you, can you, pay to these critical leadership legacy pressure points?

1. By Who Gets Promoted: An impact-rich opportunity exists with every hire and most certainly every promotion. Each new voice and behavioral model becomes a chorus for the legacy you wish to leave. Have you ensured a commitment to diversity, a system that puts the right people in the right roles at the right time? Does your organization accurately evaluate and develop employee potential? *Are you deputizing the right people? Are your leadership expectations clearly at work in promotion decisions?*

What do you do if the civil service system or other personnel system with which you work poses constraints upon you selecting the exact person you believe is the right match? Many of us have them; those systems where test scores or seniority might dictate the slate of candidates from which you must choose. Or worse, "the" candidate you must take. This can be frustrating as well as damaging to the leadership culture you wish to build. Years of experience, high test scores, or bureaucratic ability to navigate a personnel system are not customarily the evidence of leadership we look for. If indeed, your personnel system restricts your ability to "select" the candidates you consider right for leadership, then it's important to *begin ensuring that the pipeline creating candidates is preparing leaders not senior bureaucrats.* By working hard to redesign leadership development from the ground up, including having those leaders with the right leadership competencies teaching and coaching in the developmental curriculum, you begin impacting the leadership quality of candidates choosing to advance. The higher the leadership quality in the pipeline, the less retarding the selection process will be on your legacy.

- Recall the last selection you made. How will that enhance your legacy focus?
- Can you recall a selection decision that didn't support your legacy focus?
- What are the upcoming opportunities to impact your leadership legacy by a personnel selection?
- How might you enhance your "leadership development" program to ensure leaders learn twenty-first century leadership?

2. By Example: Modeling may be one of the top three teaching methods. When others see consistent leadership behavior despite the ups and downs of organizational life, they take note. Watching you navigate the narrows, deal with the setbacks, learn, and put a stake in the ground for important values teaches others what leaders do and how to do it. Trust, integrity, and commitment to others can all be taught by modeling. You don't have to go out of your way to model: you're being watched 24/7 by impressionable minds … make it count. *What do you hope people are seeing in you every single day, no matter what?*

- Reflect on your last full workweek: what "leadership" did you model?
- Did you have opportunity to "walk the talk" important to your legacy?
- Where might you need to be more alert to where your "model" is sending a message?

3. By How You Handle Crisis/Failure: The Army War College reminds us that no battle plan ever survived the first shot intact. Bad things happen to great plans and how you handle crisis when it happens leaves a deep impression on those keeping close tabs on how leaders lead. If you want people to react with the right instincts in hostile, confusing, and unpredictable moments, you have to demonstrate it yourself. These are moments and situations rich with influence potential: people are alert, seeking responsive leadership, and receptive. Leading a proper debrief after any significant action or event helps to seal in the learning.

Ernst and Andre (2006) remind us people learn best when they learn "in the moment" and that critical reflections and dialogue as we go through challenging periods helps keep the focus on improvement rather than finger pointing. *How do people describe your crisis mode? Do you ensure adequate debrief and exploration following less than optimal occurrences so people can learn?*

- Recall the last crisis or failure in your organization: what do you hope people saw in how you handled it that reflected a leadership message?
- Might they have seen anything that didn't reflect the leadership messages you desire to be sending?
- How consistently does your organization hold learning debriefs? Are they positive learning events or blame finders?

4. By consistent Messages: Effective leaders have a way of boiling down complex values, strategies, and expectations into concise elevator messages. Then, they make sure these messages are heard over and over. That welcoming presentation to new staff, the awards ceremony, a community speech, and comments while visiting a site or team meeting all offer opportunities to send, send, and resend the legacy messages you wish picked up. Redundancy is not wasted effort. Redundancy is necessary for people to hear, recognize consistency, and begin connecting the dots to their behavior and decisions. Consistency of message embeds clarity. *What are your core legacy messages?*

- What's the elevator message regarding your leadership legacy?
- Where might you find even greater opportunity for this to be heard?
- Are other organizational leaders picking up on and supporting the message?

5. By Systems and Decisions: Decisions, and ultimately the systems and protocols that support and drive them, always reflect the values and expected behaviors of the organizational culture—of the leadership climate. Your decisions and the systems you put in place are additional "models" of the leadership you seek to develop organization-wide. Fairness, empowerment, decentralization, inclusiveness, transparency, integrity, and other values are prominently displayed by systems and decisions.

- Which systems need adaptation to better align with the leadership legacy you seek to leave?
- How have your recent decisions been messages about the leadership climate you expect?
- What one decision can you make in the next few weeks to help accelerate or embed your legacy?

6. By Recognition and Appreciation: What gets noticed gets repeated. What gets repeated gets embedded. Recognition and reinforcement need to be matched to the style and sensitivities of the organization. Personal comments, thank yous, and notes of appreciation help sustain the effort. More prominent organization-wide awards become a clear message to everyone about what you believe is important. Professionals and macho organization types need this as much as anybody. While mission connectedness may be sufficient for most people to give you great performance, personal recognition is required to seal in leadership behavior. The more difficult the new behavior, the more counter to the old culture it is, the greater the volume of recognition and appreciation is needed from you.

- What strategies are you using to reinforce, recognize, and appreciate the behaviors and actions that support the legacy important to you?
- What management/leadership action have you recently recognized that is supportive of the climate of leadership/leadership legacy you desire?

- Think of other leadership activities that you may not have amply recognized that you can show appreciation for over the next few weeks.

7. By Coalitions you Form: Influence is not linear. Command is not simply hierarchical. And leadership is certainly not an individual sport. In addition to surrounding yourself with folks who compliment and enhance your own leadership impact, who have you recruited from the less obvious sectors of the organization to help give consistent voice to your legacy? Opinion leaders don't always occupy an official seat of power. They do, however, have influence power. Ensuring you have a coalition and that they feel the impact of your teaching, modeling, and communication simply distributes your legacy deeper and deeper into all the nooks and crannies of the organization. These coalitions allow you to leverage the leadership strengths others possess, demonstrate openness to influence (followership), and distribute leadership even deeper into the organization.

- What broad-based coalition can you count on to support your leadership legacy objective?
- Can you name ten non-management personnel who can be counted on to be vocal as your coalition?

8. By Teachable Points of View. Influencing values and leading with impact requires that we be clear on our own points of view and how to teach what we've learned. Teachable moments happen every day in large and small venues. If you're clear on the impact you desire to make, then you most likely can tell instructive stories, ask questions that lead others to consider implications and values, and nurture others to develop strong ideas of their own. A good storyteller tells a good story; a great storyteller helps us see ourselves in the story (Wacker and Taylor 2000).

Are you teaching? Are you purposely spending the time to explore, explain, and have others engage you about your values, style, and approaches? While it's nice to be prominent in the leadership development program in your organization, also stay aware of the teachable moments that approach us every day. Are you also cognizant and openly appreciative of what others are teaching you? If you're approaching leadership as it's written about here, you're learning enormously as you go. You can also teach by letting others see how you learn. Leading is teaching and learning. *How are you teaching? How are you openly talking about your own learning?*

- What formal and informal opportunities are you finding to teach?
- Where do those leaders who don't have day-to-day contact with you get a chance to learn from you?
- Are you certain all the management and leadership development in your organization reflects twenty-first century leadership concepts and the important elements of your legacy?
- When's the last time you thanked someone for helping you learn by giving you a teachable moment?

9. By Mentoring and Coaching: All winners have good coaches. You had natural talent but others helped you focus, refine, and polish that talent into the leader you are today. Recall our "developing others" research summary from chapter IV and never underestimate the personal mentor/coach impact. Choose those you believe have the values you wish to promulgate and the talent to learn the leadership behaviors you believe important to the future of your organization and then give them personal developmental attention. It's possible to handle three or four at a time. Yes, it takes time. However, remember your leadership mission: legacy. Great leaders have "teachable points of view" which accelerate the development of others and the organization at the same time. They also understand the two-way nature of teaching. By teaching and coaching others, leaders also become learners and grow their own ability to see the field of play and the pathways to success. Noel Tichy labels this the "virtuous teaching cycle" that winning organizations apply to continually generate more and more learning (Tichy 2003). Helping create a few more role models and several more voices for leadership will maximize the potential for your gift to take root.

- Who in your organization considers you their mentor/coach?
- How do other leaders in your organization learn to mentor/coach?
- Are mentoring and coaching commitments rewarded? How?

10. By Persistence: The will to lead frequently requires dogged determination to make the impact you envision. Neither short-term setbacks nor sluggish adopters dishearten leaders. Leaders settle in for the long run, keep their eye on the desired horizon, and tenaciously cling to making their mark through the strategies identified above. If a leaders' time is short, they focus on the vital few impacts they believe they can make in the time that they have, no excuses.

Leaders also have supporting networks that help them stay focused in the darkest of times. They hold themselves accountable despite the tension this may create with difficult leadership challenges. Leaders are also realists. Sometimes barriers and unworkable strategies need tweaking or abandoning for new strategies. Persistence doesn't mean not adjusting your strategy. Persistence means you intend to reach the destination and put your heart, emotion, and political capital on the line to do so.

- Are you persisting?
- Upon whom do you count for emotional support within the organization?
- Upon whom do you count for emotional support external to the organization?
- Persistence can be stressful. How are you managing this tension? Who can help?

Application Planning

Envision a typical day in your life as a leader.

How many of these elements will present themselves as opportunities for enhancing a leadership legacy?

How might you create an even greater opportunity to enhance your legacy through these strategies?

Look back at the planning notes you took at the end of Chapter V and see what you might add, enhance, or change.

Ensuring a Leadership Legacy Strategy: Postscript

Finding the Time

Yes, we're frequently asked during our presentations on this topic, "How does one find the time for all of this?" In a theoretical sense, the great leader makes time. In a practical sense, the great leader has clarity of focus and is more aware of all the opportunities presenting themselves every day to impact leadership legacy.

As part of achieving focus, great leaders frequently stop doing something else. That is, they are passionate about the use of their time and rabid about culling out the meetings, lesser commitments, and wasted effort that might interfere with a more efficient leadership impact. They also recognize that impacting leadership legacy, even the previous ten suggestions you've just reviewed, does not require big chunks of time all the time. Think moments. Look for the moments where the opportunity exists for an elevator message, a firm personnel decision, an extra few minutes of coaching, and a few seconds of appreciation at the end of a conversation might all align with your legacy focus. Focus on modeled behavior where every action is a leadership message. Distribute leadership to others, rally the right coalition, and maintain clarity of intentional focus on your leadership legacy and you're likely to find there's time opportunity everywhere.

CHAPTER VII

▼

TEN LEGACIES WORTHY OF THE TWENTY-FIRST CENTURY

You make a living by what you get … but you make a life by what you give.
Winston Churchill

Many of you read the heading for this chapter and probably thought, who are these guys to be nominating what my legacy should be? You would be right. Any prescriptive approach to your legacy would be arrogant and audacious because we don't live in your leadership culture with your challenges and your competency sets.

However, we have lived in contact each year for over thirty years with a multitude of organizations, leadership climates, and enterprise challenges. Those have been our work, our consulting, and our passion. From those contacts and our observations about the challenges facing leadership in the twenty-first century, we will risk stretching your thinking around what we do believe are ten crucial aspects of organizational leadership worthy of leadership legacy reflection. Are these the only ones? Of course not. One size cannot possibly fit all. However, we believe you will be able to see yourself in some small way in each of the categories discussed below. It is that reflection we seek as outcome rather than prescribing what your personal legacy focus should be.

1. **Integrity**: You only need read the headlines in the twenty-first century to determine that gross dishonesty continues to be rampant. While Enron is a massive poster child for this values deterioration, there are also matters of integrity of lesser dimensions seen in our everyday workforce. A culture of integrity also includes the little things such as rating an employee higher than you believe to

avoid wrestling with their defensiveness or not speaking the truth on the organizational survey. How are the day-to-day integrity issues being handled in your organization? Leaders give permission for people to confront organizational integrity issues and teach them how to do it with diplomacy. Simply because your organization hasn't had a newspaper headline integrity issue doesn't mean it's not worthy of re-energizing your voice.

2. **Adaptability**: In an era of ongoing transformation, leaders certainly recognize that organizational flexibility/adaptability is crucial to survive and thrive. "Successful companies, particularly those that have enjoyed a relatively benign environment, find it extraordinarily difficult to reinvent their business models. When confronted by paradigm-busting turbulence, they often experience a deep and prolonged reversal of fortune" (Hamel and Valikangas 2003). What leaders must accept is their role in helping others gain change compatibility. It's one thing to be personally adaptable, it's quite another to create a climate of leadership where everyone relishes change, has competencies to lead it, and sees value not only in evolution, but also frequent revolution. Teaching people to better anticipate change, recover from stumbles, and adapt smoothly to new demands are worthy legacies for the twenty-first century. The late Peter Drucker encouraged us several years ago to make the entire organization a change agent, not simply a few leaders at the top (Drucker 2001). His advice seems even more appropriate today and a legacy worthy of the twenty-first century. (See Chapter VIII for further elaboration.)

3. **Developing Leaders at All Levels**: We believe leadership in the twenty-first century is less about "you" as a leader and more about the "climate of leadership" you are able to create. Such a climate is distinguished by believing everyone has leadership in them and a commitment to develop leaders at all levels. In their book by the same name, Spreitzer and Quinn call this focus *A Company of Leaders* (2001). During his GE years, Jack Welch modeled this commitment by personally teaching at GE's Executive Development Center every two weeks and didn't miss a session in sixteen years. David Novak, head of Yum! Brands, committed to leading ten weeks of leadership workshops around the world and understood how important it was for growing the business (Tichy 2003). Remember, the average manager spends 15–20 percent of his or her time on employee development activities, which implies the great ones commit even more (Corporate Executive Board 2003). Look for the teachable moments that present themselves every day.

In *The Leadership Pipeline* (2001), Charan, Drotter, and Noel write about making a commitment to helping each employee with leadership transitions from individual leadership through enterprise-level leadership for those who have the will to take on that challenge. The organizations demonstrating this commitment to leaders at all levels find traditional succession planning tactics to be less critical because they always have a ready pool of capable people already leading and ready to step in when positional openings appear. (See the article in the Appendix, "Ten Pressure Points for Leadership Succession" for further elaboration.)

4. **Leveraging Diversity:** We're not certain the respect for diversity that ushered in the EEO and Equal Opportunity era has been fully realized. Even your organization may have a way to go to have a full climate of respect and inclusion for ethnicity and gender. However, a greater legacy worthy of the twenty-first century is the strategic use of difference as organizational strength. This is hard for some people to get their mind around. But as discussed earlier, leaders seek out diverse points of view, put themselves in positions to hear and learn about differences in their organizations and with customers, and ensure that diverse input is a driver of participative decision making. Such leaders also see that organizational recruitment and selection processes affirm diversity way beyond the traditional sense in order to ensure fresh thinking and perspective are brought to bear on continued organizational success. Intellectual capital resides not only in the traditional training but also in the diverse experiences of people. Twenty-first century leaders understand this and push their organizations to act to leverage this diversity.

5. **Commitment to Learning:** Leaders are learners. They never consider themselves "arrived" and seem always to be seeking new perspectives, investigating what makes others successful, and reflecting on how they are leading. This is beyond simple curiosity for hobby topics or literature of interest. This is about leaders challenging themselves and teaching the organization to challenge itself to continue reflecting, learning, and growing. When Peter Senge introduced "learning organization" into common organizational language in 1990, he recognized a commitment to learning as an organization-wide legacy worthy of effort (Senge 1990). Is there an open climate of learning, dialogue about successes and failures, and non-finger-pointing autopsies of less than optimal outcomes? Are regular critical reflections sessions (Ernst and Martin 2006) commonplace in the learning structure of your organization?

6. **Thinking Differently:** What's not working? What are your challenges? What are our weaknesses? Chances are these are the first questions you were taught to ask when you became a manager or took over a new work unit. Even if you were taught to use a full spectrum set of questions like those in a SWOT (Strengths,

Weaknesses, Opportunities, Threats) analysis, most likely you zeroed right in on the problems and weaknesses. This is not evil nor is it bad advice.

However, we propose that a twenty-first century leadership climate would benefit from looking more closely at what works and finding ways to do more or leverage that success even more. This is not about either/or focusing on problems or successes. It is about ensuring leaders are as focused on appreciating what's working well and helping the organization learn from those successes. This approach is neither new nor less developed as leadership theory than other approaches. Well articulated by Cooperrider and Srivastva (1987), its premise is that an organization that keeps focusing on problems will find more and more things that don't work well. An organization looking to discover what it's best at will continue to find more and more that is good. Leaders use appreciative inquiry as a process for engaging people across the organization around what works. This approach enhances a climate of acknowledgement of contributions and success and builds an even greater energy for success (Whitney and Trosten-Bloom 2003; Cooperrider, ed. 2004).

We're not suggesting you abandon a problem solving approach. We are suggesting that you may leave your associates an even greater legacy of leadership by asking first "What's working well?" or "What are our greatest successes?" This approach makes traditional managers and leaders nervous. We are so ingrained to study the problems that it feels disingenuous to start the other way around. It's not either/or! Can you make this a part of what you teach your organization to do? Think differently!

7. **Innovation**: A climate of creativity results in novel approaches being taken to traditional processes and products. However, a climate of innovation results in dramatic shifts in the entire model of why processes and products exist and how they should be delivered. Creativity happens much more naturally as employees and customers tinker, out of a sense of efficiency and effectiveness, with the elements of process and products. Innovation happens less naturally and requires a climate that allows organizational associates and customers to challenge the very nature of the process or product itself. As Day and Schoemaker suggest in their new book about strategic vigilance, leaders must give people permission and "the ability to always question and provide room for disproving conventional wisdom" (Day and Shoemaker 2006).

Because innovation requires significant permission, energy, and collaboration, the bigger innovation paradigm shifts are rarer than creative slants resulting in incremental changes. Permission, energy, and collaboration are the result of leadership. Think about your own organization: What big innovation has occurred in the last several years? Does your organization welcome the voice of those who think far beyond the horizon about your basic models of service and product? The contemporary organizational literature would tell us that innovation is rare and that it takes significant leadership to bring it to fruition. Because innovation is so rare, it certainly stands in our eyes as a critical nominee as a leadership legacy worthy of the twenty-first century.

8. **Transparency**: While it may be harder to keep a secret in the modern-day organization teeming with e-mail, Internet, curious unions, customer groups, and the press, it's not a good idea anyway. People have always wanted to know the ins and outs of what's happening in their place of work—both strategic and tactical—and the reasons why. It's not easy and it does take time to inform and provide rationale. However, trust, commitment, and better overall decision making at the lowest levels occur when the climate of leadership is open rather than closed. Why is this so hard? Many reasons, but we can think of several to ponder in the context of a leadership discussion. First, too many organizations model leadership that's more secretive than open because their leaders don't trust the associates with full disclosure. Additionally, ask yourself how many leaders you've known who could share openly and were capable of managing the predictably tense dialogue that goes with communicating clearly while respecting the views of all organizational associates. Not many, we would venture.

Transparency is not simply about being open; it's also about the communication competencies to navigate the organizational discussion that follows in a manner that creates common energy, trust, and resiliency. Consider the transparency proposition from where you sit in your organization. To us, it feels worthy of a leadership legacy to leave a culture capable of handling transparency.

9. **Balance**: Baby boomers are characteristically accused of letting their working years eschew balance. Millennials are characteristically labeled with caring too much about themselves and time off. In between is the proper path to navigate. We work to live, we don't live to work. The future organizational culture that finds a healthy balance and demonstrates it in policy, behavior, and leadership commitment will not only be a better place for people to work but also will be a magnet for the brightest and best.

The typical twenty-first century organization is moving fast. At speed, it's easy for leaders to overlook the human equation and potential discomfort or lack of trust involved in transformation. However, contemporary experience tells us that workers are looking for "workplaces where their feelings are treated with dignity and respect. People in pain aren't usually working at their best" (Frost 2003).

Quality of work life must contribute the balance sought by a new breed of workers or suffer from melancholy relationships, reduced discretionary effort, fewer people willing to step into leadership, and tougher recruitment and retention. If this does-n't ring true to you, it's because you're not paying attention. A twenty-first century climate of leadership is healthy, energized, and respectful of our other real life.

The new balance in the workplace is also about fun. We know the lucky among us are those who believe the "work" we get paid for is like being paid for a hobby. Year after year, the "best places to work" organizations don't simply have great ben-efits, they are also known as fun environments. Everybody enjoys an upbeat work environment and finding other fun-loving associates among their teams. Leaders who can help work feel like play help the organization garner even greater innova-tion and engagement. And then there's better recruitment and retention to boot.

When people feel respected for having a life and enjoying life even at work, the brightest and best give loads of discretionary effort. As the challenge of 24/7 work connectivity and the complexity of personal living accelerates, leaders who make an impact in this dimension of their organizational culture will surely be leaving a legacy of sizable proportion. This includes your own balance. People are watching.

10. **Giving Back**: In their book, *Claiming Your Place at the Fire*, Leider and Shapiro (2004) make the case for determining purpose in life and letting it, not your job, guide your life. Leading so that others can find their purpose and learn to follow it is both a personal and a global legacy. Leaders get to know their asso-ciates so that they know the person behind the position. Without fail, there are aptitudes, service commitments, and other outside-of-work contributions your associates are making. Find them and reward them.

Giving back in the twenty-first century has become a great deal more than making contributions to charitable organizations and initiatives. Giving back has become known as "socially responsible" as well as "eco-friendly." Corporate phi-lanthropy is now frequently embedded in the values statement and giving behav-ior of the most progressive global business organizations. While hundreds of names could be provided as example, simply check out the Web sites for Sony, Unilever, Johnson and Johnson, and RE/MAX International corporations as well as the World Business Academy and Business Alliance for Local Living Economies to understand why giving back is a corporate legacy worth leaving. Most every major business magazine now reports annually on organizations in these categories—both profit and not-for-profit—who demonstrate leadership by their awareness of and responsibility to the greater communities as well as the planet they impact (see Dahle January 2007; Engardio 2007).

CHAPTER VIII

▼

LEADING CHANGE BY CHANGING THE CONVERSATION

We, your followers, are anxious about the future. To turn our anxiety into confidence, you must tell us why we will win. You must tell us why we will prevail in this better future you seem to see so clearly.

Marcus Buckingham

We frequently shock participants in our learning seminars and keynotes by stating that people don't resist change. After a purposeful pause, we ask participants if they agree. Of course, they do not. They have story after story of associates resisting change in their organizations. We push back, challenging them to think differently. How exactly do they behave, we ask? The answers are fairly common and consistent: people gripe about leaving a process they know, and are comfortable with, for a new process; people don't believe the change is the right change; people don't trust management's intentions for making the shift; people are mad and resist because they don't feel their interests have been considered; and on and on. You know the list as well as we do.

What do all these behaviors have in common, we ask? Are they about the change itself? In some cases they are, especially when people don't agree with the direction or the new model. And obviously, when jobs go away, no one deals with that change very well. Most frequently, however, the employees' behavior is about how the organization is dealing with their issues. And when transformation is taking place, there are predictable human emotions and issues that are not "resistance" per se, but simply normal human responses.

For instance, employees may fear they cannot adequately learn a new process and don't trust that the organization will give them the training and support to

72

learn it. Around technology solutions and changes, this fear is frequent. Other employees are simply comfortable with how they do the work and where they do the work. They don't see the rationale behind changing work processes or work space and, therefore, humanly desire to stay with the comfortable and known rather than face the unknown. Other employees are angry with organizational management for "surprising" them with the change. They feel disenfranchised and are convinced the organization does not care about their ideas or emotion. In organizations where input has been sought, yet little recognition or follow-up has occurred, people come to believe it was "faked" interest in their ideas and, therefore, withdraw from supporting the change. Some people actually disagree vehemently with the direction of the change and do not wish to support the transition.

So what's common in most of the traditional responses to change? We don't believe people resist "change" as much as they resist "being changed." What we see are normal human responses deserving leadership attention. Fear, comfort, lack of understanding, lack of trust, feeling manipulated rather than involved, and being unable to see the benefit of the transformation—all of these are normal responses to changing one's life or work. If we think of these as resistance to change, our temptation is to push, prod, and pull to "overcome" resistance. It might be helpful to think a bit differently about the change phenomenon.

What we also know is that, in their daily lives, these same people change every day. They change as their family matures or divides, their economic status shifts, their social network expands, the street crew blocks a street for repair, their favorite restaurant closes, or their child gets a new teacher. What's the difference? We believe the difference is that the normal human being changes when it is in the course of natural evolution they expect and understand (e.g., kid in school, elderly parents) and/or when it's a change that has reward for them (e.g., a diet, new home, new social networks, or a new place of worship).

The human spirit deals with change fairly effectively at the adult level. In fact, when bad things happen to good people, most of us adapt and move on, because we have to, and more importantly, because we have information and choice in our responses. That we believe is the key to leading organizational change and transformation. We need to see what's in it for me. We need to be reassured that the organization understands the trepidation we have and will work to help us in the transition. We need to connect the dots to understand how the change will be helpful to the organization and what our vital role is in the new order. We need to feel someone cares about our ideas about how to make the change orderly or even better than originally designed. We need to feel we're not being changed, but instead, we are being respected as an integral part of the change and treated likewise.

Yes, we are aware that a small percentage of the workforce does actually resist change because they disagree with the rationale and can't buy into the benefits the organization sees. We also understand that downsizing, moving employees, and needing to move with dispatch with some change will not be palatable to any of us; it hurts too much. However, if we focus on the 90 percent or greater of our workforce who will cooperate with us and the 20 percent or so of that group who have wished for some of these changes for a long time, we have an opportunity to help organizations achieve ongoing transformation more smoothly and with more intellectual capital engaged in the process.

Great leaders, we find, attend to two critical elements of leading change. One, they create a culture of ongoing dialogue about the future so that conversations are occurring regularly about how the organization, department, or work might need to adapt to changing conditions and expectations. These discussions don't require committees or hours of meetings. Transformational leaders embed these conversations in existing meetings and conversations with organizational opinion leaders and set aside some time each quarter to have a "futures discussion." A workforce engaged in thinking about the future, examining customer, citizen, economic, technological, and values shifts around their enterprise grows more alert to the need for ongoing transformation and becomes much more change compatible.

Second, effective transformational leaders ensure that the organization invests in answering the four critical questions that our associates have about any change:

1. Why do we need to change?
2. Where will this take us?
3. How will we get there?
4. What's my role?

Let's explore these in more detail.

Leading Change by Sharing the Story of Interest to ME!

Effective leaders are generally recognized as more adept at anticipating needed transitions/transformations and communicating the need to change in a manner that allows people to know all there is. While sharing objective data and transition plans won't always engender full-boar support for a change effort, it is something that can be done that at least creates an opportunity for people to opt in.

We know in any change effort there are the early adopters, possibly up to 15 percent who see the field immediately (Rogers 2003). Once leaders share the rationale, the destination, and the migration map, this group begins to move and has energy around the change. Many in this group wonder what took you so long to see the need to move.

The next 30 percent are the slower adopters who need to mull over the case for change and reassure themselves that the journey has been well planned and the destination has a reasonable chance of success. They will join in reasonably soon and are frequently most convinced not by the formal organizational leaders, but by the opinion leaders among their groups. This group also needs to hear the "change" messages repeated and repeated.

Another 30 percent will grumble, stumble, and possibly hope until the last light is turned off that they really don't have to invest in this change. Most of them will eventually go along and not sabotage the efforts. These last two groups are why change efforts require redundant communication of what's going on. Some people need to hear and hear it again before it sinks in.

The last 20 percent may fight you all the way, some will even actively sabotage, and all will most likely be vocal as any calamity hits the change effort. These may be the same 20 percent whom the Gallup organization brands as "actively disengaged" (Buckingham and Coffmann 1999)

For the last 50 percent of the folks buying into the change effort, it's important to communicate small wins as they occur as a means of neutralizing some of their fear and grousing. With that perspective in mind, let's look more closely at the answers leaders must provide in their messaging (stories) about change.

Why Change?

- What's so bad about how we are doing now?
- What aspect of our business environment is forcing us to adapt?
- What's going to be better?
- If we wait a while and work hard, won't the need go away?
- Have we been performing badly?
- Exactly how do shifting trends and external expectations impact us?
- What's the gap between where we are and the business environment expectations?

What's the story? These are the questions on the minds of your constituents. Yes, frequently the story is, "Our performance has not met expectations and new models are called for." More frequently, in well-led organizations, the message is more about adaptation that rescue. Witnessing shifting business conditions, the leaders recognize the adaptation required to keep the organization or department relevant, valuable, and vibrant. Can you tell a story that highlights the urgency for change? Remember, in their personal lives, people are accustomed to changing when they have a good reason, a self interest. Why is the organization any different?

> *"While a good storyteller tells a good story, a great storyteller helps you find yourself in the story."*
>
> *The Visionary's Handbook* (Wacker and Taylor 2000)

Where/What Are We Changing to?

- What's the new model/process/destination look like?
- Can you describe it to me? In detail? What will success look like?
- Has anyone else done this? Can you show me a successful model?

We are all suspicious to some extent. We don't like to go on trips to secret destinations and we are suspect of leaders who don't detail the new destination of our change effort. Change leadership can potentially be more effective when we can clearly articulate what the new model will look like once we arrive or at least give a high-level architecture to it. Answers to the "where are we going" questions are as important to the adult employees in your organization as they were to your childhood trip in the family car. In the case of children, it's curiosity and excitement driving the question. In the case of your organizational associates, it's concern about how well we might have thought out where we are going and whether they can see some semblance of connection between the "why" we're moving and the "where" we're moving too. Articulate a "vision" of a new, more desirable organizational position (structure, service/productivity, and relationship with stakeholders and customers) and provide us as much detail as possible about the blueprint.

How Are We Going to Get There?

- What's the implementation plan?
- What are the milestones? How fast or slow will we need to go?
- What if I need training and development to learn to work in the new situation?
- How will we measure progress?
- What will happen if I can't keep up?

Most people don't like to go on a secretive journey they know nothing about. They enjoy even less not knowing what the map looks like. Many of us have been through less than optimal change efforts in our careers. And many of us have learned that the planning of how to get from old to new is critical to peace of mind and a pain-free journey. Those late adopters who don't jump right in? Frequently, it's because they don't trust that organizational leaders have a plan. Letting people see, hear, and touch the plan gives greater confidence to those who didn't want to move in the first place and helps reduce anxiety all around. Yes, some will disagree with the plan. Others will offer great advice. But all will benefit from knowing the path we plan to take and the milestones expected along the way. A clear roadmap facilitates early adopters' journey speed, reduces later adopters' journey anxiety, and allows both skeptics and cynics to sanity check our plans. These are all healthy elements of a leadership climate.

Addressing the change "map" allows the organization to demonstrate it has thought through needed re-learning that may be required along the way. It also allows the organization to point out key forks in the road where input will be required. At the outset, a high-level map is all that is usually needed. Fretting Fred and Phyllis will always desire greater detail, but at least they can see the field rather than being surprised. And guess what? If you've missed something important, your associates have a chance to provide some good intelligence about the proposed journey.

Finally, a story relevant to me provides clear expectations about me personally. What do you need from me during this change effort?

What's My Role?

- What exactly do you need me to do? How will I be measured?

- Do you want to hear how I feel, what I think, or if I see something going wrong?

Fear of performing is one of the greatest retarding emotions. Help people know how you will support them, how they will be measured, and what help you need from them as we all undertake the journey.

Conversations with early adopters simply ask, "What do you need?" Conversations with later adopters offer clarification, encouragement, and teaching. Conversations with diehards and doubters demonstrate appreciation for not sabotaging the effort and empathize with their criticism while reaffirming where we are going and our current progress.

Putting It All Together

People generally don't resist change. They change every day. They do bristle at being left out of the conversation, they may fear the new future, and they can be skeptical of our ability to foresee a correct future and deploy a safe and successful journey for them. They also rightfully expect an honest attempt to fully disclose the organization's intentions. That's what we believe.

The Four Key Questions approach does not intend to downplay the complex psychology of leading change, nor the significant strategic and tactical planning necessary for successful change. We do intend to suggest that the communication of change leadership be guided by messages that answer the key questions posed here.

John Kotter reminds us in his seminal book *Leading Change* (1996) that most organizations under communicate the change message by a factor of at least ten. Your leadership team must scope and harness the key answers to the change questions and repeat those messages until they become the common conversations throughout the organization about your change venture. Then, you will have communicated enough.

CHAPTER IX

▼

LEAD FROM WHERE YOU ARE

We must be the change we want the world to see.

Ghandi

It's a lot, we know. The more we read the literature articulating how leadership is developing and impacting organizations in the twenty-first century, the more wonder we have for the vastness of it all. At times, the success of some leaders seems superhuman and at other times we look with awe at the simplicity of how some leaders create strength from limited platforms. It is enough to be tempted to declare, "I got here okay, so I must be doing fine" and not challenge yourself to learn and focus even more. But that's not what great leaders do. Remember also, great leaders don't do it all and are not all competent across the full spectrum of leadership capabilities.

We take encouragement from a simple story, told so many times by motivational speakers that it risks emptiness to those who hear it again. A young person walks on the South Florida shore pitching back into the ocean starfish that have washed ashore by the hundreds. An older person approaches the youngster and calls attention to the numbers of starfish on the shore, suggesting the tyke can't possibly make a difference. After a moment considering the advice, the young person picks up a starfish, tosses it into the ocean, turns, and exclaims, "There, I made a difference for that one, didn't I?"

We suggest you take council from this metaphorical story. Sometimes a little is a lot. Simple can be powerful. Simply taking the first step changes the equation. While it's nice to have visions of your future leadership position and opportunity, it's important that you not overlook the present for its own opportunity. One of the best nuggets of management advice that we've received reminded us to "Do the best job you can in the job you're in, and the future will take care of itself."

Provide the opportunity to grow, reach out to others, and contribute to a climate of greater leadership right where you are.

Here are some final thoughts about leading where you are.

If You're Not Yet in a Managerial Position

Should you even be thinking about leadership, much less legacy impact here? We think yes, and here's why. Leaders consistently demonstrate that they can help people and organizations become successful wherever they are. Leaders are learners and are constantly striving to learn how to be more successful themselves. So, yes, your behavior makes a difference to your team and, to an extent, effective leadership behavior at this level models (teaches) others how they can also lead. Facilitating teamwork, problem solving, and innovative thinking is leadership as is raising ethical concerns and seeking clarity about strategy. Clarifying expectations for the team and helping others navigate difficult work challenges is leadership. So first, recognize that these leadership behaviors at the team level are your learning/proving ground for potential next levels of leadership. Others aren't looking to see how well you "boss" others. Your boss and others are watching to see how well you help others be successful.

Because leaders are learners, you should be actively involved in self-assessment and development. Don't wait for the organization to do this for you. Take your own initiative. Get a learning coach/mentor. Engage in self assessment about your own emotional intelligence and interpersonal competency. Emotional Intelligence (EI) is a platform for whatever other leadership opportunities you might find: learn about it and practice improvement (Goleman 1995). Feedback is a gift and it's important to listen carefully to the impressions of others about your behavior. Set your own development plan and ask your immediate boss and others for assistance. Find learning opportunities within and outside your work environment to test your leadership skills at this level.

As importantly, make sure you are absolutely clear about performance expectations and that you focus on delivering with excellence. Clarity is a most critical accelerator of success and your fundamental work success at this level is the foundation for any future leadership opportunity you might get.

Some Helpful Readings:
  Change the World: How Ordinary People Can Accomplish Extraordinary Results (Quinn 2000)
  Emotional Intelligence (Goleman 1995)

"How to Play to Your Strengths" (Roberts 2005)
Now Discover Your Strengths (Buckingham 2001)
"Personal Histories" (HBR Survey 2001)
The Highest Goal (Ray 2004)
The Oz Principle (Connors 2004)
The Seven Habits of Highly Effective People (Covey 1989)

If You're a New Leader

Can you remember the doubts and hopes you had for new managers who came into your work life? If so, you're well on the road to knowing how to take on the new leader role. Leadership is grounded in relationships and trust. Unless there's some crisis (see later section of this chapter), people don't care how much you know until they know how much you care. Take the time to work one-on-one with each individual directly reporting to you, getting to know their work, their concerns, and their ideas for a better workplace. Discover each individual's unique talent and interests and look for ways to leverage them for both the individual and the organization. Encourage each of their visions of personal success.

In the spirit of appreciative inquiry, find out what people believe is working well and ask them how you can help them make it work even better. Looking for the positive is always a nice start to a leadership climate and allows people to show you their passion, interests, and knowledge all at the same time. See your job as helping your associates be as successful as possible and continually ask, "What do you need from me?" Be careful about trying to be the source of all wisdom and heroically pushing too hard right away. When you behave by trusting and seeking input, you build trust for the moments when you may need to nudge behavior, performance, or goals. Remember the new managers you've had in your career: didn't you hope they would come in and take the time to appreciate the contributions you were already making? We believe so, and therefore, we urge you to mark your legacy by creating a climate where your can facilitate people reaching for the stars.

Beginning a new leadership relationship in this manner allows you to leverage the caring teacher approach. Recall that coaching and developing others is found in the research to be one of the top three most powerful leadership competencies. People respond well to someone who cares about them and their success and contributes to success in a manner that makes them stronger.

Some Helpful Readings:
  A Company of Leaders (Spreitzer 2001)
  First Break All the Rules (Buckingham 1999)
  "How to Play to Your Strengths" (Roberts 2005)
  It's Your Ship (Abrashoff 2002)
  Learning Journeys (Goldsmith 2000)
  The Magic of Dialogue (Yankelovitch 1999)
  The Real Work of Leaders (Laurie 2000)
  Thin Book of Appreciative Inquiry (Hammond 1996)

If You're an Entrenched, Longer-Term Leader

Certainly, consider what legacy you've been leaving during your tenure. How do people characterize the leadership climate? How many other leaders have you developed and moved on in the organization? Innovation, balance, transformation, and integrity—how prominent are these characteristics in your team? Using our thoughts on twenty-first century leadership, self-assess where you've built strength and how you can leverage that strength to even greater success. Using the same assessment, can you see possibilities for targeting new legacies?

It's not unusual for long-term leaders to face complacency—theirs and others—and to be satisfied with continual incremental improvement in their achievements. We're not saying that's bad. We are asking, where's the passion? What is it that might drive your enterprise/team to even greater success? What can energize the team to see new possibilities and believe in even greater success in their future?

If you're a long-term leader facing the need to re-energize your organization, a few questions might guide your focus. Are you having regular ongoing conversations about adaptive challenges ahead in your business environment? Is there a common energizing view of your future? Are there a clearly identified "vital few" strategic objectives that will change the level of energy and feelings of success? Leveraging these areas can give exciting direction and motivation to a team challenged by complacency.

How well are you building leadership in others? Possibly you could re-energize the leadership development process and your own commitment to it. When you change the conversation about what leadership is, how we're leading, and how we're growing as leaders, you also change the organizational climate.

Entrenched, long-term successful leaders must frequently challenge whether they are simply performing well or great. We believe great leadership comes from a commitment to continual self-assessment and learning both for you as an individual leader as well as for the organization as a whole. If coming to work everyday and solving problems is your passion, congratulations. You're most likely a very successful manager. However, we challenge you to think more radically about leadership in the twenty-first century and your passion for it. What's the climate of leadership you're leaving as a legacy to those who look to you to distribute leadership? Will people say, "We did fine"? Or, will people say, "We learned to be great"?

Some Helpful Readings:
Growing Your Company's Leaders (Spreitzer 2004)
Inevitable Surprises (Schwartz 2003)
Leading the Revolution (Hamel 2000)
Peripheral Vision (Day 2006)
The One Thing You Need to Know (Buckingham 2005)
The Power of Impossibly Thinking (Wind 2004)
Visionary's Handbook (Wacker 2000)
Whoosh (McGehee 2001)

If You're a Leader Facing Extraordinary Challenges

Leaders confront reality and the reality is that most organizations are facing enormous challenges as they navigate the future. You may be leading in an organization for which the challenges are extraordinary and feel overwhelming. You're not alone. We work with hundreds of leaders like you every year that are not at this crossroad because they were poor leaders, but at this crossroad because today's challenges demand greatness in leadership. The external environment is becoming more and more unforgiving.

Thomas Friedman reminds us in *The World is Flat* (2005) that "change is hard"; however, "change is hardest on those caught by surprise." In the twenty-first century, the leader facing extraordinary challenges must ensure that a candid sense of urgency is understood by all. Transformation must be put in the perspective of the types of changes going on in the business environment. Jim Collins (2005) found that "great leaders confront the brutal facts." Are you certain that all organizational associates see and understand the facts of your changing business environment? That's the foundation for gaining discretionary effort, tapping motivation for survival, and giving people a common challenge to conquer rather than simply marching faster because you say so. Ask yourself how well you've created that "sense of urgency" (Kotter 1996). Look back at the guidance we suggest in Chapter VIII and change the conversation about needed transformation.

If you can create a leadership climate where ongoing conversations about the future occur with regularity, then at least you're creating a legacy where people can be more self-sufficient about anticipating the future rather than depending on you. If the challenges are indeed extraordinary and you and the organization are feeling the stress of the transformation curve, then you might look around you and find a strong coalition of the willing in whom you can distribute leadership. Great odds are not conquered by single-minded heroes. Extraordinary challenges require a crew all synchronized and pulling in the right direction. Ensuring the right coalition of leaders throughout the organization, all with the same passion about leading through the challenges, helps teach the organization to depend on a climate of leadership rather than a single leader. That's a worthy legacy, because we all know other extraordinary challenges will be around the corner and we don't need associates who sit around waiting to be told what to do by the "leader."

Frequently, the biggest dilemma with overwhelming challenge is determining where to start. It may look so foreboding that the average manager can wilt in the vastness of it all. We believe twenty-first century leadership targets a vital few pressure points and works to create breakthrough results on those as a means of overcoming inertia. Success breeds success, and visually seeing movement eroding away the extraordinary challenges energizes the entire organization and leads to even greater success.

The twentieth century leader was frequently taught to create a "burning platform" from which people would be forced to leap onto the "new architecture" or process. While fear is a great motivator, we believe twenty-first century leadership conquers extraordinary challenges by helping people clearly see the reality of the status quo, fully participate in setting a common energizing vision, and directly stimulate the leadership they can all bring rather than being rescued by a heroic leader.

Perfect strategies and tactics inevitably will not overcome extraordinary challenges. Leading through these challenges may require recovering from lots of missteps and wrong assumptions. Teaching people that they can learn and recover from these less than optimal outcomes embeds a sense of can-do leadership deeper and deeper into the organization. Leaders don't see failure, they see lessons. Leaders recognize that much of life, and a lot of organizational life, is recovering from the latest series of oversight, slips, and falls. That's not failure in our book.

As creatures of our past—our past managerial and heroic success—we will all be tempted to rescue and or manage people harder as a means of surviving extraordinary organizational challenges. Admitting this and catching yourself is the first step in learning to lead in the twenty-first century. Grinding on people as a means of burrowing out from under a challenge is not only old school, it's less integrity in human relations than we should accept. Don't be tempted.

Some Helpful Readings:
Critical Reflections (Ernst 2006)
Failing Forward (Maxwell 2000)
It's Your Ship (Abrashoff 2002)
Leading Change (Kotter 1996)
Peripheral Vision (Day 2006)
"*Tipping Point Leadership*" (Kim 2003)
Visionary's Handbook (Wacker 2000)
"*Your Company's Secret Change Agents*" (Pascale 2005)
12: The Elements of Great Managing (Wagner 2006)

If You're a Second-in-Command Leader

Frequently, the second-in-command leader is the operations person. That is, they are tasked with more day-to-day oversight of processes and deliverables than strategic thinking or external relationship building. Whatever the focus your boss asks of you as the second in command, we believe all the characteristics of twenty-first century leadership prove relevant.

Every leader needs someone who is confident enough to disagree with them. All leaders seek the candid voice of fresh thought, alternative options, and hypotheses for what's happening—diplomatically, of course, but candid nonetheless. Learning to disagree with diplomacy, influence without authority, and garner trust even when being a discordant voice models behavior for other leaders and brands you as a broad-spectrum thinker.

Despite the need to bring fresh perspective, you are also the voice of the leadership vision and values. The second in command is most frequently supportive of vision and values by being a consistent voice as he or she navigates day-to-day operations. Because you may have greater one-on-one contact with associates not in formal leadership roles, your voice becomes critical to keeping focus and goals alive.

Whatever the profile asked of you as second in command, please stay focused on you as a leader. Look for the leadership moments in everything you do. Developing others, mentoring, and assisting others in finding learning opportunities are all moment-to-moment elements of leadership that don't require lots of extra time. Building trust among associates and enhancing communication that enables successful performance by others are all legacy impacts that occur moment to moment. But don't forget about your own development. As second in command, you're in a great position to challenge yourself to grow and find greater opportunities for leadership. Rather than simply looking to the hierarchy for leadership opportunity, look deeply within yourself for changes that you may need to make to leverage your strengths, add new capabilities, and gain broader organizational perspective.

The role you play in helping others navigate your boss is an additional opportunity for leading and teaching. Facilitating upward communication, helping others maintain focus, coaching others on diplomatically bringing different ideas to the marketplace, and modeling political savvy all help and teach others at the same time. Talk about all of this learning with your mentor.

Some Helpful Readings:
Deep Change (1996)
Influence without Authority (Cohen 2005)
Leading with Questions (Marquardt 2005)
Leading Quietly (Badaracco 2002)
Learning to Lead (Bennis 2003)
"*Second in Command*" (Bennett and Miles 2006)

If Your Current or New Manager Doesn't Buy Twenty-first Century Leadership

If everybody got it, we wouldn't need to keep talking about it. You will report to those, and work with others, who don't understand or believe the elements we've written about as twenty-first century leadership. There will be plenty of folks who disdain transparency, leading vs. managing, and committing to the diversity of thought that strengthens organizations. Remember one critical thing about heroic leaders or competent managers who aren't leaders: the integrity of your relationship with them and with your team is yours to own. No one can sour the trusting, open, and coaching relationships you form with others. Bad bosses can make it more difficult to commit to lead in a twenty-first century manner, but they cannot prevent you from the integrity of your relationships. Relationships are yours to own.

Working for and with leaders who are stuck in the old school requires patience and political savvy. When you're trying to lead differently than those around you, the commitment to "no surprises" is more critical than in other circumstances. Keep people apprised and explain the rationale for the leadership tactics and strategies you choose. Help others focus on your accomplishments and what you deliver, rather than whether you did it similar to how they would have done it. Carefully pick your issues, ideas, and how you push back, because you're at greater risk here.

What are your manager's critical pressure points? Can you demonstrate effectiveness on those issues while using twenty-first century leadership? If so, you'll be given some slack and quite possibly model behavior that other leaders can pick up. Delivering well in the job you've been given has always been the safest path to building credibility. And yes, even old–school, traditional managers have learned a thing or two about leadership by watching their direct reports achieve success with twenty-first century leadership approaches.

Being open while reporting to a manager who doesn't believe in the twenty-first century leadership path can be both risky and helpful. Clearly indicating to your manager that you mean no disrespect but see your role as helping to ensure that all decisions and approaches are thoroughly vetted might provide some amnesty for challenging the way he or she is leading. Try to contract with your manager about the importance of your role in asking questions. Not questioning to be disruptive, but questioning to open lines of sight and ensure thorough validation of decisions and approaches. We know seeking to formalize this role can be risky with managers who still believe everyone should just do what they say. We also believe that choosing not to try to change the conversation and the relationship is not leadership—survival possibly, leadership, no.

Whatever level of wiggle room you can eke out, leading in a more open and progressive manner can still feel lonely within this environment. Look for others who understand your commitment and leadership approach and work with them as a supportive coalition. Together you may have greater impact on demonstrating that twenty-first century leadership works. Certainly, a supportive coach or mentor can also be instrumental in helping you navigate these waters and provide a safe outlet for talking through your frustrations. And when, despite your best efforts, it's an unfulfilling effort working for someone who cannot buy into twenty-first century leadership, don't be afraid to seek a different venue. Resolute effort to be effective in such a climate is honorable. Eternal suffering is not helpful to your growth or your own future, so seek out new opportunities with courage.

Some Helpful Readings:
Leading Quietly (Badaracco 2002)
Influence without Authority (Cohen 2005)
The Seven Secrets of Influence (Zuker 1991)
Leading With Questions (Marquardt 2005)
How to Stubbornly Refuse to Make Yourself Miserable (Ellis 2006)

If You're a Committed Leader

No matter where you find yourself as leader and regardless of the endless theoretical and strategic recommendations you get about leadership (from us and others), please try to remember that if you live a life of learning and values, you will have less to fear from disorder. If you can live a life with focus, you will have less to fear from uncertainty. Leaders choose their path by recognizing their passion, growing their capabilities, and having clarity about their intended impact. Finally, no matter where you are, please take encouragement from eleven-year-old Nkosi Johnson's charge to leaders everywhere:

> Do all that you can.
> With what you have.
> In the time that you have.
> In the place you are.
>
>   Xolani Nkosi Johnson, 1989–2001

References and Other Helpful Readings

Abrashoff, Captain Michael. *It's Your Ship*. New York, NY: Time Warner, 2002.

Albrecht, Karl. *The Northbound Train*. New York, NY: AMACOM, 1994.

Lulthans, Fred, and Bruce Avolio. *The High Impact Leader: Moments Matter in Accelerating Authentic Leadership Development*. New York, NY: McGraw Hill, 2006.

Avolio, Bruce, and Bernard Bass. *Developing Potential Across a Full Range of Leadership: Cases on Transactional and Transformational Leadership*. Mahwah, NJ: Lawrence Erlbaun Associates, 2002.

Badaracco, Joseph. *Defining Moments: When Managers Musts Choose Between Right and Right*. Boston, MA: Harvard Business School Press, 1997.

Badaracco, Joseph. *Leading Quietly: An Unorthodox Guide to Doing the Right Thing*. Boston, MA: Harvard Business School Press, 2002.

Bennett, Nathan, and Stephen Miles. May, 2006. "Second in Command: the Misunderstood Role of the Chief Operating Officer." *Harvard Business Review*.

Bennis, Warren, and Burt Nanus. *Leaders: The Strategies for Taking Charge*. New York, NY: Harper Row, 1985.

Bennis, Warren. *Learning to Lead: A Workbook on Becoming a Leader*. Cambridge, MA: Basic Books, 2003.

Bennis, Warren, Gretchen Spreitzer and Thomas Cummings, eds. *The Future of Leadership: Today's Top Leadership Thinkers Speak to Tomorrow's Leaders*. San Francisco, CA: Jossey-Bass, 2001.

Boyatzis, Richard, and Annie McKee, *Resonant Leadership*. Boston, MA: Harvard Business School Press, 2005.

Brooks, Martha, Julie Stark, and Sarah Caverhill. *Your Leadership Legacy: The Difference You Make in People's Lives*. San Francisco, CA: Berrett-Koehler Publishers, 2004.

Buckingham, Marcus, and Curt Coffman. *First Break all the Rules: What the World's Greatest Managers Do Differently.* New York, NY: Simon and Schuster, 1999.

Buckingham, Marcus, and Donald Clifton. *Now Discover Your Strengths.* New York, NY: The Free Press, 2001.

Buckingham, Marcus. *The One Thing You Need to Know … About Great Managing, Great Leading, and Sustained Individual Success.* New York, NY: The Free Press, 2005.

Byham, William, Audrey Smith, and Matthew Paese. *Grow Your Own Leaders: How to Identify, Develop and Retain Leadership Talent.* Upper Saddle River, NJ: Prentice Hall, 2002.

Charan, Ram, Stephen Drotter, and James Noel. *The Leadership Pipeline: How to Build the Leadership Powered Company.* San Francisco, CA: Jossey-Bass, 2001.

Cohen, Allen, and David Bradford, *Influence without Authority.* Hoboken, NJ: John Wiley and Sons, 2005.

Collins, Jim. *Good to Great.* New York, NY: HarperCollins Publishers, 2001.

Colvin, Geoffrey. October 19, 2006. "What it Takes to Be Great." *Fortune Magazine.*

Connors, Robert, Tom Smith, and Craig Hickman. *The Oz Principle.* New York, NY: Penguin Group, 2004.

Cooper, Simon. December, 2005. "He Who Says It, Does It." *Business 2.0.*

Cooperider, David, and Suresh Srivastra. "Appreciative Inquiry in Organizational Life." W. Pashmore and R. Woodman, Eds. *Organizational Change and Development.* Greenwich, CT: JAI Press, 1987.

Cooperrider, David. *Appreciative Inquiry: Rethinking Human Organization Toward a Positive Theory of Change.* Champaign, IL: Stipes Publishing, 1999.

Corporate Executive Board. 2002. "Closing the Performance Gap." Catalog No. CLC1W10HS.

Corporate Executive Board. 2003. "Employee Performance Improvement: Understanding Your Role as a Manager." Catalog No. TD11A8Q65.

Corporate Executive Board. 2003. "Hallmarks of Leadership Success." Catalog No. CLC11Q0U3L.

Corporate Executive Board. 2003. "Engaging Managers as Agents of Employee Development." Catalog No. TD11IMXNC.

Corporate Executive Board. 2004. "Driving Performance and Retention Through Employee Engagement."

Corporate Executive Board. 2005. "Unlocking the Full Value of Rising Talent."

Corporate Executive Board. 2006. "Leaders Who Develop Leaders."

Covey, Stephen. *The Seven Habits of Highly Effective People: Restoring the Character Ethic.* New York, NY: Simon and Schuster, 1989.

Dahle, Cheryl. January, 2007. "The Fast Company/Monitor Group Social Capitalist Awards: A More Powerful Path." *Fast Company.*

Dauphinais, G. William, and Colin Price, Eds. *Straight From the CEO: The World's Top Business Leaders Reveal Ideas That Every Manager Can Use.* New York, NY: Simon and Schuster, 1998.

Day, George, and Paul Schoemaker. *Peripheral Vision: Detecting the Weak Signals That Will Make or Break Your Company.* Boston, MA: Harvard Business School Press, 2006.

DePree, Max. *Leadership is An Art.* New York, NY: Doubleday, 1990.

Dotlich, Donald. *Unnatural Leadership.* San Francisco, CA: Jossey-Bass, 2002.

Drucker, Peter. *The Effective Executive.* New York, NY: Harper Row, 1967.

Drucker, Peter, and Joseph Maciariello, *The Effective Executive: A Journal for Getting the Right Things Done.* New York, NY: HarperCollins Publishers, 2005.

Drucker, Peter. November, 2001. "The Next Society—Survey of the Near Future." *The Economist.*

Effron, Marc, Robert Gandossy, and Marshall Goldsmith, Eds. *Human Resources in the 21st Century.* Hoboken, NJ: John Wiley and Sons, 2003.

Ellis, Albert. *How to Stubbornly Refuse to Make Yourself Miserable About Anything: Yes Anything.* New York, NY: Kensington Publishing Company, 2006.

Eiser, Barbara, A. Eiser, and M. Parmer. March/April 2006. "Power of Persuasion Influence Tactics for Health Care Leaders." *Leadership in Action.*

Engardio, Pete. January 29, 2007. "Beyond the Green Corporation." *BusinessWeek.*

Ernst, Chris, and Andre Martin, *Critical Reflections: How Groups Can Learn from Success and Failure.* Greensboro, NC: Center for Creative Leadership, 2006.

Leigh, Davie, and Alan Leigh. *The Corporate Fool.* Oxford, UK: Capstone Publishing Ltd., 2001.

Friedman, Thomas. *The World is Flat.* New York, NY: Farrar, Straus and Giroux, 2005.

Frost, Robert. Fall , 2003. "The Hidden Work of Leadership." *Leader to Leader.*

Fulmer, Robert, and Jay Conger. *Growing Your Company's Leaders.* New York, NY: AMACOM, 2004.

Gardner, John. *On Leadership.* New York, NY: The Free Press, 1993.

George, Bill. *Authentic Leadership: Rediscovering the Secretes to Creating Lasting Value.* San Francisco, CA: Jossey-Bass, 2003.

Gladwell, Malcolm. *The Tipping Point.* Lebanon, IN: Little, Brown and Company, 2000

Goldsmith, Marshall, Beverly Kaye, and Ken Shelton. *Learning Journeys.* Palo Alto, CA: Davies-Black Publishing, 2000.

Goleman, Daniel. *Emotional Intelligence: Why It Can Matter More Than IQ.* New York: NY: Bantam Books. 1995.

Gosling, Jonathan, and Henry Mintzberg. November, 2003. "The Five Minds of a Manager." *Harvard Business Review.*

Hamel, Gary. *Leading the Revolution.* Boston, MA: Harvard Business School Press, 2000.

Hamel, Gary, and Liisa Valikangas. September, 2003. "The Quest for Resilience." *Harvard Business Review.*

Hammond, Sue. *The Thin Book of Appreciative Inquiry.* Bend, OR: Thin Book Publishing Company, 1996.

Handy, Charles. *Beyond Certainty.* Boston, MA: Harvard Business School Press, 1996.

Handy, Charles. *The Age of Paradox.* Boston, MA: Harvard Business School Press, 1994.

Handy, Charles. *The Age of Unreason.* Boston, MA: Harvard Business School Press, 1990.

Harvard Business Review Survey. December, 2001. "Personal Histories: Leaders Remember the Moments that Shaped Them." *Harvard Business Review.*

Heifetz, Ronald, and Donald Laurie. January, 1997. "The Work of Leadership." *Harvard Business Review.*

Hesselbein, Francis, Marshall Goldsmith and Richard Beckhard, Eds. *The Leader of the Future.* San Francisco, CA: Jossey-Bass, 1996.

Izzo, John, and Pam Winters. *Values Shift: The New Work Ethic and What It Means for Business.* Vancouver, BC: FairWinds Press, 2001.

Kim, W. Chan, and Renee Mauborgne. April, 2003. "Tipping Point Leadership." *Harvard Business Review.*

Kotter, John. *Leading Change.* Boston, MA: Harvard Business School Press, 1996.

Kouzes, James, and Barry Posner. *A Leader's Legacy.* San Francisco, CA: Jossey-Bass, 2006

Kouzes, James, and Barry Posner. *Credibility.* San Francisco, CA: Jossey-Bass, 2003.

Kouzes, James, and Barry Posner. *The Leadership Challenge.* San Francisco, CA: Jossey-Bass, 2002.

LaFasto, Frank, and Carl Larson. *When Teams Work Best.* Thousand Oaks, CA: Sage Publications Inc., 2001.

Laurie, Donald. *The Real Work of Leaders.* Cambridge, MA: Perseus Publishing, 2000.

Leider, Richard, and David Shapiro. *Claiming Your Place at the Fire: Living the Second Half of Your Life on Purpose.* San Francisco, CA: Berrett-Koehler Publishers, 2004.

Leonard, Dorothy, and Walter Swap. *When Sparks Fly: Igniting Creativity in Groups.* Cambridge, MA: Harvard Business School Press. 1999.

Lopez, Anthony. *The Legacy Leader: Leadership With a Purpose.* Bloomington, IN: Anthony Lopez, 2003.

Luthy, John. 2000. "Leaving a Leadership Legacy." *Public Management.*

MacKenzie, Gordon. *Orbiting the Giant Hairball.* New York, NY: Viking Penguin, 1996.

Martin, Andre. September/October, 2006. "Rules of Engagement: Trends That Could Change the Landscape of Our World." *Leadership in Action.*

Marquardt, Michael. *Leading with Questions: How Leaders Find the Right Solutions by Knowing What to Ask.* San Francisco, CA: Jossey-Bass, 2005.

Maxwell, John. *Failing Forward: Turning Mistakes into Stepping Stones for Success.* Nashville, TN: Thomas Nelson Inc., 2000.

McGehee, Tom. *Whoosh: Business in the Fast Lane, Unleashing the Power of a Creation Company.* Cambridge, MA: Perseus Publishing, 2001.

Meyer, Paul. *Unlocking Your Legacy: 25 Keys for Success*. Wheaton, IL: Tyndale House Publishers, 2002.

Nkosi (Xolani Nkosi Johnson), www.simplytaty.com/bios/nkosi.htm

Oakley, Ed, and Doug Krug. *Enlightened Leadership: Getting to the Heart of Change*. New York, NY: Fireside, 1991.

Pascale, Richard Tanner, and Jerry Sternin. May, 2005. "Your Company's Secret Change Agents," *Harvard Business Review*.

Partnership for Public Service and the Institute for the Study of Public Policy Implementation. 2004. "The Best Places to Work in the Federal Government." www.bestplacestowork.org.

Peters, Tom. *Thriving on Chaos: Handbook for a Management Revolution*. New York, NY: Alfred A. Knopf, 1987.

President's Management Agenda. 2002. www.whitehouse.gov.

Quinn, Robert. *Deep Change*. San Francisco, CA: Jossey-Bass, 1996.

Quinn, Robert. *Change the World: How Ordinary People Can Accomplish Extraordinary Results*. San Francisco, CA: Jossey-Bass, 2000.

Ray, Michael. *The Highest Goal: The Secret that Sustains You in Every Moment*. San Francisco, CA: Berrett-Kohler, 2004.

Ridderstrale, Jonas, and Kjeell Nordstrom. *Funky Business*. London, UK: BookHouse Publishing, 2000.

Morgan-Roberts, Laura, et. al. January, 2005. "How to Play to Your Strengths." *Harvard Business Review.*

Rogers, Everett. *Diffusion of Innovations*. New York, NY: The Free Press, 2003.

Rutzick, Karen. January 23, 2006. "Employees Keep Training Expectations to Themselves." www.govexec.com.

Senge, Peter. *The Fifth Discipline: The Art and Practice of The Learning Organization*. New York, NY: Doubleday, 1990.

Schwartz, Peter. *Inevitable Surprises: Thinking Ahead in a Time of Turbulence*. New York, NY: Bantam Doubleday Dell, 2003.

Schwartz, Peter. *The Art of the Long View*. New York, NY: Gotham Books, 1991.

Schon, Donald. *Beyond the Stable State: Public and Private Learning in a Changing Society*. New York, NY: W.W. Norton and Company, 1973.

Secretan, Lance. *Inspire! What Great Leaders Do*. Hoboken, NJ: Wiley, 2004.

Spence, Linda. *Legacy: A Step-by-Step Guide to Writing Personal History.* Athens, OH: Swallow Press, 1997.

Spreitzer, Gretchen, and Robert Quinn, *A Company of Leaders: Five Disciplines for Unleashing the Power in Your Workforce.* San Francisco, CA: Jossey-Bass, 2001.

Sull, Donald. March, 2006. "Difficult Decisions for an Uncertain World." *Financial Times.*

Thomas, David, and Robin Ely. September/October, 2003. "Making Differences Matter: A New Paradigm for Managing Diversity." *Harvard Business Review.*

Tichy, Noel. Summer, 2003. "Getting the Power Equation Right." *Leader to Leader.*

Tichy, Noel, and Mary Anne Devanna. *The Transformational Leader.* New York, NY: John Wiley and Sons, 1990.

Tichy, Noel, and Eli Cohen. *The Leadership Engine.* New York, NY: HarperCollins Publishers, 1997.

Trinka, Jim. 2004. "Building Great Leadership at the IRS." *Industrial and Commercial Training.* Volume 36, No. 7.

Trinka, Jim. 2005. "What's a manager to do?" *Industrial and Commercial Training.* Volume 37, No. 3.

Trinka, Jim. July, 2005. "Great Leaders." *Leadership Excellence.*

Trinka, Jim. September, 2005. "What's a Manager to Do?" *Leadership Excellence.*

Trinka, Jim. May 22, 2006. "What leaders need to do." *Federal Times.*

Useem, Michael. *The Leadership Moment.* New York, NY: Random House, 1998.

Vaill, Peter. *Learning as a Way of Being: Strategies for Survival in a World of Permanent White Water.* San Francisco, CA: Jossey-Bass, 1996.

Wagner, Rodd, and James Harter. *12: The Elements of Great Managing.* New York, NY: Gallup Press, 2006.

Wacker, Watts, and Jim Taylor. *Visionary's Handbook.* New York: NY: Harper Business, 2000.

Weiss, Jeff, and Jonathan Hughes. March, 2005. "Want Collaboration? Accept and Actively Manage Conflict." *Harvard Business Review.*

Wheatley, Margaret. *Leadership and the New Science.* San Francisco, CA: Berrett-Koehler, 1999.

Whitney, Diana. *The Power of Appreciate Inquiry: A Practical Guide to Positive Change.* San Francisco, CA: Berrett-Koehler, 2003.

Wind, Jerry, Colin Crook and Robert Gunther, *The Power of Impossible Thinking: Transform the Business of Your Life and the Life of Your Business.* Upper Saddle River, NJ: Wharton School Publishing, 2004.

Wooten, Jim. *We Are All the Same: A Story of A Boy's Courage and A Mother's Love.* New York, NY: Penguin Press, 2004.

Yankelovitch, Daniel. *The Magic of Dialogue.* New York, NY: Simon and Schuster, 1999.

Zenger, Jack, and Joe Folkman. *The Extraordinary Leader.* New York, NY: McGraw-Hill, 2002.

Zuker, Elaina. *The Seven Secrets of Influence.* New York, NY: McGraw-Hill, 1991.

Appendix 1: Signature Resources Leadership Competencies

Competency	Leadership Outcome
Vision	*New Desired Future*
Critical, Strategic Thinking	*Seeing Future Opportunity*
Creating and Energizing Vision	*Energizing a Future Story*
Adaptation/Transformation	*Remaining Relevant*
Leading Transitions	*Helping People Cope*
Leading Work Process/Systems Redesign	*Improving Work Process*
Sponsoring Continuous Learning	*New Knowledge Applied*
Facilitating Creativity/Innovation	*Breakthrough Ideas*
Developing Partnerships, Alliances, Coalitions	*Influence/Strength*
Developing Leaders at Every Level	*Taking Responsibility*
Distributing Accountability for Outcomes	*Better Employee Decisions*
Creating Involvement in Decision Making	*Employee Ownership; Creativity*
Developing/Leading "Cellular" Multifunctional Teams	*Fluid, Flexible Teams*
Leadership Development	*Growing the Next Generation*
Leveraging Diversity	*Ideas; Creativity*
Communication	*Clearer Information & Goals*
Openness/Transparency of Information	*Access to Information People Need*
Coaching/Mentoring	*Teaching, Growing Employees*
Influence/Negotiating	*Selling Ideas; Reduced Conflict*
Interpersonal Competence (Emotional Intelligence)	*Strong Relationships*
Customer Focus	*End User Gets Value*
Client Value & Satisfaction Measures	*Earlier Diagnosis of Trouble*
Products/Services Designed with Customer Input	*Improved Value*
Quality Improvement	*Reduce Mistakes/Waste*
Self	*Integrity/Credibility*
Values/Ethics	*Trust, Respect*
Continuous Learning	*Intellectual/Emotional Growth*
Personal/Professional Balance	*Family Life and Work*

Appendix 2: Ten Pressure Points for Leadership Succession

With Frank Benest
(City Manager, Palo Alto, California)

We have a caution for the current wave of "succession planning" angst setting in as government and business are challenged by the many baby boomers leaving their employment soon. Traditional succession planning has focused on charts with names of potential temporary or permanent successors for a key vacancy. This is good thinking for the most part. However, it may not be as robust an investment as a progressive twenty-first century enterprise should be making.

"Leadership succession," a more recent development of traditional succession planning, focuses on an enterprise-wide development of leaders at all levels so that the organization can be confident a capable pool of talent is constantly being readied to compete for positions as they open. Rather than focusing only on "replacement" (succession) and targeting a limited one or two names, leadership succession invites many to identify their interest in possibly moving up and becoming involved in leadership development. This process is more inclusive (read fair), transparent (rather than secretive), and, when done right, becomes an accelerator for organizational success.

Candidates who choose not to compete for more responsibility or those who don't compete successfully still benefit (as does the organization) from what they've learned. In short, more people win. As Jim Collins' most recent research (*Good to Great* 2001) indicates, "Great companies grow their own and they do this with a broad-spectrum leadership development investment long term rather than episodic succession management exercises."

While the contemporary literature is replete with recommendations and models for succession planning, we offer the following ten considerations as strategic thoughts for creating a leadership succession culture in your organization.

1. **Invite all employees to express their interest in leadership development and begin growing them accordingly.** Inviting folks to identify their interest in frontline, midlevel, and senior/executive level leadership offers an "inclusive" rather than "exclusive" approach to a talent pool and helps ensure greater objectivity in finding and developing talent. Every organization is at risk of only seeing selected favorites as the next generation of leaders. Every organization also has a talented pool of leaders possibly not getting the break they need and who will grow immensely when given fair opportunity to develop. Allow learning and performance to differentiate who continues to move up rather than isolated views or pre-selection of one or two managers. While your organization may be well beyond the "good ole girl/boy" selection process, a more inclusive talent development approach ensures more riches available to drive success.

2. **Target readiness programs for each specific level of leadership.** Employees who feel they might be interested in frontline management should experience "readiness" learning events that help them decide if management is for them and, if it is, begin learning the basics. At the appropriate time, frontline managers should be able to experience a similar readiness program for mid-level management and similarly for increasing levels of leadership. This might be as simple as a two-hour brown bag lunch and learn on "What it means to be a manager" or as intensive as a couple of days overview and introduction to what it means to be a manager, replete with self-assessments, in-basket exercises, and case studies. Potential candidates better informed about the reality of the job and the leadership competencies required will likely make more rational individual decisions about choosing the next level of leadership. It also helps to discourage those not serious or simply fantasizing that they have the right stuff when possibly they don't. (See attached Figure 1 graphic of readiness & development sequences.)

3. **Ensure a robust leadership development program grounded in competencies across all levels of organizational leadership.** Defining the appropriate leadership competencies for your organization is a required starting point for twenty-first century leadership development. IBM and Bank of America have recently refreshed their expected competencies to better align with today's business environment. The U.S. Office of Personnel Management has twenty-eight competencies organized within five executive core qualifications used by federal agencies for development and selection criteria. Typical competencies include "leading change and transformation," "collaboration and building coalitions," "leveraging diversity," and "developing others."

Identifying and articulating leadership competency behaviors most critical to your enterprise will take work, but it will ensure you are providing leadership learning in your programs *and* targeting the most crucial competencies for your organizational success. Smaller organizations will also benefit from competency development because they will be in a better position to outsource learning engagements or direct candidates to the most appropriate individual learning opportunities. One of the most up-to-date treatments of leadership competencies, *The Extraordinary Leader* (Zenger and Folkman 2002) is a good starting point as well as an excellent refresher for those less familiar with leadership competency models.

Escalating your leadership development program to the equivalent of an "academy" or "university" is both very possible and encouraged for larger organizations. The investment will return valuable dividends and there are numerous models from which you can custom design your own. While a formal leadership development program might reside in human capital departments, recognize it is the responsibility of the entire executive cadre to oversee development, deployment, and evaluation of such a program.

4. Recognize that talent development is a primary role, of equal importance to other leadership/management tasks. One of the more urgent roles of today's manager/leader is that of "talent manager." If this long-term developmental role is not a primary responsibility, it will get shoved aside by urgent, shorter-term challenges. However, if talent development is defined as important and expected, it will occupy time and attention as a significant function. "Developing others" is commonly recognized as one of the most critical twenty-first century leadership competencies. Is this competency prominent in your expectations for all levels of management? Are appropriate level coaching and mentoring skills required competencies to move up in your organization?

5. Give aspiring leaders a broad range of technical and interim assignments. The private sector does this best, but the public sector can also accomplish this if made a priority. Acquiring broad-based experience provides up and coming leaders a big-picture view of the enterprise and helps them connect the dots to the value of various functions and tasks. Additionally, varied experiences also provide a vibrant real-world laboratory for applying newly learned leadership and management competencies. Leaders who see the "portability" of their learning and demonstrate success no matter where they work will likely compete more strongly for the next promotion and add greater value when promoted than a leader with narrower experiences.

If formal job placement can't be navigated through your personnel system, then try temporary assignments to other functions for shorter periods of time, e.g. one week to three months. Aspiring leaders can "act" temporarily while other managers are out or fill an interim appointment while a position is being backfilled.

6. Deploy participants in readiness and management development programs on special projects across the organization. Often, talented, up and coming leaders are assigned only to support roles or special-project teams in their current work unit or division. Having them serve as fresh eyes or staff resources for a broader multi-departmental initiative or project stretches their ability to apply competencies in new settings and gain intellectual peripheral vision regarding the enterprise. Loaning a readiness participant short-term to operational initiatives in other work units broadens business literacy and whole organization perspective. The networking, collaboration, and leadership experience in a different setting are invaluable to professional growth and benefit the candidate and the organization long term.

7. Accelerating strengths rather than focusing on weaknesses. Yes, we believe in this controversial approach, much promulgated by the Gallup organization from its employee engagement and development research work (*Now, Discover Your Strengths* 2001) and further reinforced in other contemporary literature (*The Extraordinary Leader* 2002). We're not talking here about overlooking core requirements for levels of leadership. A mid-level manager unable to effectively manage budgets and financial planning, an executive unable to think strategically, and a frontline manager unable to manage performance each has a significant shortcoming that, left unaddressed, will lead to failure. However, if the competency meets requirements, but is not the strongest competency, effort elsewhere in the developing leader's portfolio of strengths is likely to return the biggest dividends. In general, effective leaders gather their strengths together and make them even stronger in order to make their weaknesses irrelevant. Think about the best leader you've worked for or with. He or she had weaknesses, but his or her few strengths overshadowed them. If we set the bar adequately for minimal capabilities, then we need not worry about making every capability a strength. Every effective leader has weaknesses.

8. Voluminous and candid feedback. A 360-degree feedback approach for all participants in leadership succession programs, done regularly, is currently the benchmark for helping candidates see themselves and their performance through the eyes of the entire organization. This helps identify and appreciate strengths. It also helps coaching feedback should any fatal flaws or serious gaps appear in a candidate's readiness. Unfortunately, the inability of the leadership development system to give candid feedback about serious inadequacies is a common shortcoming in many leadership development programs. While only a small percentage of managers are likely to have fatal flaws, those that do need to understand why they are unlikely to progress. Additionally, managers who may have moved up easily under an earlier set of promotion processes or leadership expectations deserve to know that past behavior may not meet current standards. It's not unusual for candidates not getting selected, for example, to not get honest feedback about why they weren't chosen. Not only is this a matter of integrity, it's also a matter of helping people gain confidence in the leadership development and selection processes.

We should all examine our development programs to see how honestly we help candidates become aware of serious shortcomings. Program leaders and coaches must have crucial and courageous conversations with candidates to ensure they are not blind to behavioral flaws that are likely to interfere with their ability to compete successfully for positions of greater responsibility. Then, of course, we should prescribe development action and support that will help the candidate learn new behavior. Those who desire to advance but have serious deficiencies need both candid feedback as well as caring support for growing if they so choose.

9. Focus on experiential learning, not solely traditional classroom education. While many organizations still promote classroom "training" as the primary means of developing leadership capacity, the contemporary evidence is that adults learn best by doing. Classroom education is excellent for introducing concepts and theoretical frameworks for leadership. Experiential learning (e.g., special projects, interim positions, and stretch assignments) is the best way to create new skills and competencies. Understand this cannot be done with a zero-risk ethic. Organizations must recognize that some trial and error is inherent in the strength of action learning. There is simply no growth without mistakes. Providing robust coaching support for learners ensures that fatal mistakes don't get made, that missteps are tolerated, and that less than optimal outcomes become framed as great learning. Talent development in the twenty-first century is not focused on classroom training, but rather is a series of challenging experiences coupled with candid performance feedback. Realign your developmental template and the climate of organizational coaching to this model and leadership growth is accelerated beyond what classroom activities could ever accomplish.

10. Align all organizational systems to promote leadership succession. Leadership succession and/or leadership development cannot be isolated as an organizational initiative nor delegated to the human capital or learning and education units. When all managers accept leadership development as a function for which they are accountable, the more successful overall leadership development will be. When this interdependent alignment is realized, leadership succession begins to take care of itself as cadres of leaders continue to be ready to compete for new positions.

What do we mean by interdependency and organization-wide alignment? Ask yourself some questions. Do organizational values support upward mobility? Do annual work plans for employees at all levels include a mandatory learning or growth development plan? Is it robust or sophomoric as are many current developmental planning responsibilities of managers? Is there an expectation of cross-functional collaboration in providing action learning and interim appointments as learning opportunities? Do managers at all levels act as coaches across departments and divisions in support of developing leaders? Does the performance tracking and compensation system reward managers who develop talent? Are new managers selected based in part on their commitment to this organization-wide alignment to promote leadership succession? These are some of the many aspects of aligning organizational systems and ensuring the culture fully supports the value of a vigorous and inclusive leadership succession approach.

The Opportunity

Baby boomers are indeed leaving their organizations a legacy. Not only their years of vital service and leadership, but also by virtue of the enormous numbers ready to retire, they have inadvertently caused a global wakeup call regarding leadership succession. We can take this opportunity and simply manage it with technical management succession planning. Or, as we encourage, we can create lasting organizational value by seeing the bigger leadership succession picture and revitalizing leadership development at all levels—a leadership legacy.

Leadership Development

Targeting Strategies & Readiness for Each Leadership Level

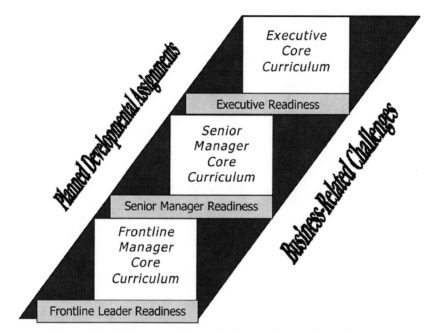

Figure 1: Typical Framework for Leadership Readiness and Development

About the Authors

Les Wallace, Ph D

Les Wallace is president of Signature Resources Inc., an international leadership and strategy firm based in Colorado with offices in Europe and Asia. Dr. Wallace is recognized for tracking business environment and workplace trends and their impact upon business and government. Drawing upon professional experience as a university professor and health care administrator, Dr. Wallace mixes practical solutions to today's organizational challenges with leading-edge ideas that stretch thinking about designing our future. Since founding Signature Resources in 1982, his workshops, seminars, and speaking engagements have reached 20,000 people a year in both the private and public sector. Active in the World Future Society and the World Business Academy, Dr. Wallace also serves on the board of directors of Counterpart International, a global economic development and relief organization, and on the faculty of the Institute for Global Chinese Affairs at the University of Maryland, College Park.

Jim Trinka, PhD

Jim Trinka is the technical training director for the Federal Aviation Administration (FAA), where he is establishing a systematic and continuous career learning and development strategy for critical occupations in the Air Traffic Organization. He also oversees the development and implementation of an integrated workforce plan to hire and train twelve thousand new air traffic controllers over the next several years. Dr. Trinka previously served as the FBI's Chief Learning Officer and managed the prestigious FBI Academy for special agents, the National Academy for state and local law enforcement officers, the Center for Intelligence Training for intelligence career service personnel, and the Leadership Development Institute. He implemented training initiatives critical to the FBI's efforts to strengthen its intelligence workforce, build on its counterterrorism expertise, and prepare agents to deal with future global threats. Prior to the FBI, Dr. Trinka served as the IRS's Director of Leadership and Organizational Effectiveness where he developed programs that continue to serve as benchmarks for both public and private institutions. He began government service with a distinguished twenty-two-year career as a fighter pilot in the U.S. Air Force, garnering many awards and distinctions. Dr. Trinka holds a doctorate degree in international politics from George Washington University and has authored numerous works on leadership development and political science.

You may contact the authors, Les Wallace (les@signatureresources.com) or Jim Trinka (JTrinka@cox.net) or through our web site www.SignatureResources.com.